The Ageless Self

Life Course Studies

David L. Featherman
David I. Kertzer
   General Editors

Nancy W. Denney
Thomas J. Espenshade
Dennis P. Hogan
Jennie Keith
Maris A. Vinovskis
   Associate General Editors

The Ageless Self

Sources of Meaning in Late Life

Sharon R. Kaufman

The University of Wisconsin Press

The University of Wisconsin Press
2537 Daniels Street
Madison, Wisconsin 53718

3 Henrietta Street
London WC2E 8LU, England

Library of Congress Cataloging-in-Publication Data
Kaufman, Sharon R.
    The Ageless self.
      [Life course studies]
      Bibliography: pp. 199–204.
      Includes index.
      1. Gerontology—United States. 2. Aged—Psychology.
    3. Self perception. I. Title. II. Series.
    HQ1064.U5K38   1986   305.2'6   86-40053
    ISBN 0-299-10860-0   ISBN 0-299-10864-3 (pbk.)

To the memory of my grandparents

FREYDA KAUFMAN
1884–1971

BERNARD KAUFMAN
1884–1973

NELLIE PINCUS
1894–1971

JOSEPH PINCUS
1894–1977

How I rejoice
            in everything around me:
My circular glass stairway,
My tiers of books,
The very rug I walk on.

It is as though with age
I had been given new eyes,
And all the common-place
Turns special.

Colors are pennants,
Curtains, golden gauze
The knobs of doors
Shape to my hands.

All rivals all in giving.

FLORA J. ARNSTEIN,
age 99

Contents

Acknowledgments

I am grateful to the 60 people who participated in the research on which this book is based. They generously opened their doors and their lives to me and responded thoughtfully and enthusiastically to my questions. They taught me much about aging and the meaning of the life course. One aim of this book has been to bring their perspectives to a wider audience.

This book began as a doctoral dissertation at the University of California, San Francisco/Berkeley. My oldest and deepest debt is to my teacher and friend, Margaret Clark. I have been extremely fortunate to work with her over the years. Her own work in the anthropology of aging inspired me to undertake this study in the first place. She encouraged and supported me in all phases of my research. She, more than anyone else, has impressed me with the importance of studying the relationship between cultural patterns and individual lives.

Gerald Berreman and Christie Kiefer also guided me through the initial research period. Discussions with them helped me formulate my ideas and expand the scope of my research. Their respective visions of anthropology have helped to shape my own.

The initial research was financially supported by a National Institute on Aging Traineeship Award (#AG-00045). Parts of Chapters 1, 2, and 5 first appeared in "Cultural Components of Identity in Old Age: A Case Study," *Ethos* 9(1) 1981, pp. 51–87.

I am indebted to several readers who made detailed comments on the manuscript. Without David Plath's encouragement, suggestions, and hard work on my behalf the dissertation would not have developed into a book. I have been deeply influenced by his work. His ideas about pathways, particularly, inform the entire book, especially Chapter 6. Roger Sanjek made astute criticisms which helped me clarify my ideas, especially on the subject of methods and life-history research. Jennie Keith, David Kertzer, David Featherman, and Bob Rubinstein all made suggestions which I have incorporated into the final version. Ellen Hershey's skill and advice have gone beyond the role of editor and have enabled me to become a better writer.

Two special friends and colleagues, Gay Becker and Deborah Gordon, have provided support in immeasurable ways. I am grateful to them for our countless discussions over the years about anthropology and gerontology, research and writing.

Carroll Estes, Director of the Institute for Health & Aging, UCSF, where I now work, gave me the freedom and support to complete this project. I thank the institute staff, especially Norton Twite and Susan Churka-Hyde, for their assistance with word processing.

Finally, I offer my warmest thanks to my husband, Seth, for his humor and perspective, and to my children, Sarah and Jacob. Their births and young lives coincided with this project, and their presence and love have made me aware of the miracle of the entire life course.

San Francisco   Sharon R. Kaufman
January 1986

The Ageless Self

One

Agelessness, Identity, and Themes

> Believing, with Max Weber, that man is an animal sus-
> pended in webs of significance he himself has spun, I take
> culture to be those webs, and the analysis of it to be
> therefore not an experimental science in search of law
> but an interpretive one in search of meaning.
>
> CLIFFORD GEERTZ, *The Interpretation of Cultures*

The process of growing old has been scrutinized by social scientists for the past 40 years and described by novelists, poets, and playwrights for at least several hundred years before that. Yet not much has been written about aging by the elderly themselves, those who know the most about it.

Now, as the largest segment of the U.S. population enters middle age, questions of how to cope with an aging population as well as with one's own later years arise from people in all age groups and from many sectors of American life: how to stay healthy and vital longer; how to provide and pay for services for those who are ill, disabled, or homebound; how to take the nightmarish quality out of the nursing home; how to maintain a decent standard of living after retirement;

3

how to generate meaning in the last decades of life; how to best channel and articulate the voices of older Americans so that their needs may be understood and met by a society that has always been youth oriented. These are only some of the questions that now face our society, and they exist because of a gap in knowledge, experience, and priorities. For though we have increased the length of our life spans through the enormous efforts of medicine, science, and technology, we have not, as a nation, channeled equal energy into defining the nature of these added years or creating positive roles and meaningful institutions through which they may be enjoyed. This lag between the added years themselves and our knowledge of how best to spend them generates numerous social and cultural problems for those who are old now and those who will be old in the coming decades.

The research upon which this book is based grew out of my awareness of this gap, the uncharted territory in which we find ourselves both as aging individuals and as an aging nation. In order to improve the quality of life experience for those in their later years, we must understand what it means to be old, to be at the end of the life cycle and have 70 or more years of experience upon which to reflect. For only by first knowing how the elderly view themselves, their lives, and the nature of old age can we hope to fashion a meaningful present and future for them and for those who follow.

Old age in American society means the period of life following the 65th birthday. Old age has been defined in chronological terms since the passage of social security legislation in the 1930s, and being old has come to be associated with predominantly negative stereotypes—decline, loss, and disease. Because of all the assumed losses—reduced sensory awareness, deaths among relatives and friends, lowered social and economic status due to retirement, for example—aging is often viewed as negative and problematic. A corollary to this negative approach is that old people live in the past rather than in the present, that personal reminiscence and historical events are more relevant and more important to them (not to mention more pleasant) than are current concerns and future prospects. Scholars interested in aging have tended to view old age in terms of loss and decline as well. Much of adult-development theory conceives of the life course as a trajectory: a person "rises" and develops by gaining knowledge, skills, roles, power, and self-esteem, and then "declines" by losing some or all of these attributes. The aging individual is often viewed as attempting or even struggling to hold onto or maintain his or her resources and morale in the face of the inevitable fall.

In the trajectory paradigm, chronological age is the critical variable: the 65th birthday marks the probable beginning of the downhill fall. With decline, loss, and chronological age as primary concerns, specialists in aging have sought to describe and understand the exact nature of the losses—be they physiological, psychosocial, economic, political—and how the losses are related to chronological age. Over the years, gerontological researchers have documented the many negative changes associated with late life with the goal of understanding the problems and needs these changes cause. And, they have identified the needs of the elderly in such contexts as biological functioning, psychosocial adjustment, health care delivery, and community involvement. Thus, many aspects of the aging process are now well understood.

In the effort to define and understand the negative dimensions of growing old and how these dimensions relate to one another, researchers have focused on component parts of the aging person and his or her life context. As researchers have concentrated on parts of the whole, the essential humanity of the older lives under scrutiny is deemphasized, is barely visible beneath research results, or is lost altogether.

I wanted to look at the meaning of aging to elderly people themselves, as it emerges in their personal reflections on growing old. This kind of inquiry requires the investigation of individual experience rather than the investigation of specific research variables. It requires looking at old people's accounts of the life course, rather than employing theoretical concepts (such as trajectory) to explain the nature of the aging process. My method was to gather data on old people's views of their lives and to concentrate on the ways in which they interpret their experience. My goal was to study aging *through* the expression of individual humanity. *The old Americans I studied do not perceive meaning in aging itself; rather, they perceive meaning in being themselves in old age.*

Efforts to understand the dimensions of meaning in old age led me to investigate the interplay between change and continuity in the individual life. Many researchers have noted that mental health depends upon ensuring a continuous sense of self across the adult life span.[1] In her now classic study of culture and aging, Margaret Clark (1967, [Clark and Anderson] 1967) discovered that old people in American society are thwarted in their expression of continuity of self by a society that makes rigid and contradictory demands for profound change among its oldest citizens. She found that individuals who could not alter, reinterpret, or reevaluate their orientation to both self and social world in old age had more likelihood of psychiatric hospitalization than those who were able to shift orientations. I discovered in my research that though sociocultural demands for change are inevitable in late life and do present dilemmas of being and action, people, in describing the meaning of their lives, are able to create continuity of self. This process enables them to cope with demands for change and, thus, is a critical resource for remaining healthy.

The Ageless Self

The voices of individual old people can tell us much about the experience of being old. In the process of conducting anthropological fieldwork with the elderly, I have heard many old people talk about themselves, their pasts, and their concerns for the future. I have observed that when they talk about who they are and how their lives have been, *they do not speak of being old as meaningful in itself*; that is, they do not relate to aging or chronological age as a category of experience or meaning. To the contrary, when old people talk about themselves, they express a sense of self that is ageless—an identity that maintains continuity despite the physical and social changes that come with old age. Old people know who they are and what matters to them now, and, as they talk about these subjects, they may, in passing, describe themselves as "feeling old" in one context and "feeling young" or "not old" in another. This is always variable, and in my experience, it is never emphasized. Being old per se is not a central feature of the self, nor is it a source of meaning. The following comments, from 8 individuals, exemplify how the ageless self was expressed by 60 people whom I interviewed about aging.

MARTHA, AGE 70

SK: Do you feel differently about yourself now than when you were younger?

MARTHA: I don't think I've ever shifted. I mean my idea of myself when I was five years old I'm quite sure was the same as it is now.

No, my sense of identity hasn't changed. Jack and I met when we were 20, and we wanted to do more or less the same thing. We were extremely sure of ourselves. . . . Then, I had children and devoted those years to them and acted the mother. I was really playing a role. But Jack and I had a very strong joint identity to return to when they left home.

SK: How have you been the same since you were five?

MARTHA: My decisiveness I guess. I can't remember ever being in a quandary or feeling that my choices were ambiguous. I really can't. I'm sure there were many times, but it seems to me that it's always perfectly clear what I should do next. . . . Also, my manner of being at home in the world. It's just how I arrived apparently. I've always felt that way. In fact, I'm very brash. Not very tactful. It's all part of that. Just a feeling I'm right.

sK: What's the hardest thing about growing older?

MARTHA: Oh, I think the physical disabilities. The aches and pains. When you come up against some that don't have any very easy remedies, you have to sit down and just make do with those things from then on, and it's not fun. Pain. Having to put up with arthritic pain. We both have arthritis.

But, we are financially secure. And we do have an enormous amount of fun. We still enjoy things.

sK: Do you feel 70?

MARTHA: I don't feel 70. I feel about 30. I wear my hair the way I did then. I notice a lot of women wearing their hair now as they did when they were about 30.

I just saw some slides of myself and was quite taken aback. That couldn't be me. That's a nice looking woman, but it couldn't possibly be me. Even though I look in the mirror all the time, I don't see myself old.

It is a bit odd now. When I used to ride the bus for a nickel, the driver used to ask to see my ID. Now, he doesn't ask. He *knows* I'm over 65.

IDA, AGE 92

sK: Tell me about being old.

IDA: There's this feeling of being out of one's skin. The feeling that you are not in your own body. I find myself acting in unfamiliar ways. Doing things that aren't familiar to me. And generally, having an outlook that doesn't seem to be my usual outlook. In a kind of way, disoriented, but I just don't know how. It's difficult to say. It's like memory lapses. You know it's there, but you don't know how to get at it.

sk: Do you feel differently about yourself now, than when you were younger?

ida: No, not too differently from the way I felt before. Except that I tire more readily. But the fact is, one isn't a different person, though perhaps some personality traits do become more pronounced.

I always think of myself as younger, though not at any specific age, just at some time in the past. Whenever I'm walking downtown, and I see my reflection in a store window, I'm shocked by how old it is. I never think of myself that way.

MAX, AGE 78

sk: Do you feel differently about yourself now than when you were younger?

max: I don't think so. Psychologically, I don't think I'm radically different than I was when I was a young man. I haven't got the fire and ambition that I had in those days, but outside of that, I don't think I'm radically different.

sk: When did you stop having fire and ambition, do you think?

max: Oh, fairly recently, when our law firm broke up.

sk: How do you know you are growing old?

max: Well, in recent years, our children have become a little more solicitous of our well-being and comfort, and so forth. My son and son-in-law will never let me pick up a suitcase when we travel. Which is an indication that we're getting older. Our children and grandchildren are very, very attentive to us. Very loving. I think that's the most gratifying part of getting older.

SARA, AGE 81

SK: What's the hardest thing about growing older?

SARA: To tell you the truth, I never noticed it until I had to use the cane. I never really noticed it. I didn't realize I was getting older. But now, I can't hide the symptoms with that damn cane. This blasted stick. You know what hurts most—my vanity. . . . I happen to be a little bit vain.

On my 80th birthday everybody made a fuss, and I couldn't imagine why. You see, most of my close friends, my contemporaries are gone, and I have sort of drifted in with younger people. I like it better. I still feel young in spirit. I can't stand being with old people, some of them are dead and don't know it. All they talk about is their illnesses, from head to foot. You never ask them how they are because they'll tell you. It's so boring.

PERCY, AGE 92

SK: What has changed about you over the years?

PERCY: Well, in the last 20 years, I've had a bad knee. That's made me walk with a cane, so I look like a cripple. I'm not a cripple mentally, I don't feel that way. But I am physically. And I hate it. I dislike it very much—not being able to walk as rapidly as other people do. That's one thing that upsets me. And uh . . . I probably try to hide it occasionally (laughs).

SK: Do you think there is anything you can do about it to be less upset?

PERCY: Well, I try to forget it. Yeah. You know, when I hear people, particularly the gals and ladies, their heels hitting the pavement, I can always tell when a woman is coming along, you know. I feel so lacking in assurance—why can't I walk that way? I feel a little bit ashamed, you know

what I mean? I shouldn't say ashamed, maybe inadequate, because I can't keep up with the others. . . . I don't like to be
looked upon as a cripple. That's the answer. Because I don't
feel like a cripple, but physically I am. Whether I like it
or not.

sk: What other ways do you think you've changed over the
years?

percy: Well, of course, some people think I'm an old cur-
mudgeon. An old codger or whatever. But to myself I don't
feel like it.

sk: Do you think of yourself as 92?

percy: No. I have the same attitude now, toward life and
living, as I did 30 years ago. That's why this idea of not being
able to walk along with other people—I'm more slowed
down—it hurts my ego. Because inside, that's not really me.

SAM, AGE 81

sk: Do you feel differently about yourself now than when
you were younger?

sam: I can see that there are certain traits in me that have
carried through from youth to now. A conservative attitude,
a wish to conform to the law, to pressures. And, I've always
been cheerful. I still am. I mean I don't wake up with a
gloomy or grumpy attitude. And I do like to be busy; I have
always been friendly. I still feel that way.

sk: Has 81 years been a long time?

sam: No, I don't think so. I will be 82 this summer and I
can't believe it. And I can think that that's because the pattern of my life has been kept so active. And if you're interested, the years fly by. No, it hasn't seemed long. It only
seems a puzzle that I'm still here (laughs). Oh dear.

ETHEL, AGE 84

SK: I want to know what it feels like to be over 70.

ETHEL: I'm not over 70. People tell me I look 60 or 65. And I feel like that too. I don't feel over 70 (presents a picture of herself at age 29).

SK: Do you relate to that woman?

ETHEL: I feel the same now as I did then, oh yes. The only way I know I'm getting old is to look in the mirror. But I've only *felt* old a few times—when I'm really sick.

You know, people say that all old people do is talk about their memories and the past. Well, I don't do that. Don't say that about me. I think about the future and tomorrow. You can't do anything about the past.

GERTIE, AGE 89

SK: How's your health right now?

GERTIE: My health is pretty good right now, thank God. I have arthritis in my shoulders. That hurts—it hurts like hell. I get pills for that. For my leg I get a water pill. But that's all I get. So, that's not bad for an 89-year-old woman.

SK: How does it feel to be 89?

GERTIE: Well, I'll be honest with you. I might be 89 years old. I feel good. I feel like I could fly the coop. I do. I feel younger, like I'm 45 or 50. I want to doll up, and I like to fuss. Oh, golly, I can break the mirror. I don't know I'm old. I feel like I'm going to live for a long time.

Martha reports that she has had the same "sense of identity" over her lifetime, which she describes in terms of her "decisiveness" and her "manner of being at home in the world." These aspects of her self, she feels, have remained constant amid changes over the course of her life: her involvement during one period in the role of mother; the "aches and pains" she must now cope with; the changes in her physical appearance and her difficulty in accepting them; the fact that others now perceive her as old. Ida, too, feels that in old age "one isn't a different person, though perhaps some personality traits do become more pronounced." She identifies changes she is coping with: a sense of disorientation, and disassociation from her body; "having an outlook that doesn't seem to be my usual outlook"; her shock at how old she looks. Yet in some way she feels that she is still the same person.

Max reports that he no longer has the "fire and ambition" he had as a young attorney. He identifies the way his children treat him as "an indication that we're getting older." Yet he says, "Psychologically, I don't think I'm radically different than I was when I was a young man." Sara, far from identifying herself as an old person, reports that she resisted that realization until she had to use a cane. She still feels "young in spirit." Percy, struggling with a bad knee, feels "inadequate, because I can't keep up with the others"; but "inside, that's not really me." He has "the same attitude now, toward life and living, as I did 30 years ago." Though his bad knee may be affecting his body image and his sense of competence in the world, he expresses a concept of a "real me" that continues to be Percy. Sam sees that "there are certain traits in me that have carried through from youth to now." His chronological age holds little significance for him: he "can't believe it." For Ethel and Gertie too, chronological age holds little meaning. Though both are dealing with the physical changes of old age, they report that they feel younger than they are.[2]

Contrary to popular conceptions of old age, which tend to define it as a distinct period in life, old people themselves emphasize the continuity of the ageless self amid changes across the life span. Old people do not perceive meaning in aging itself, so much as they perceive meaning in being themselves in old age. Thus, my initial question about the meaning of aging evolved into an inquiry into identity, or the ageless self, and how it operates as a source of meaning in old age. In asking this question, this book explores an under-investigated dimension in research on aging: rather than focusing on the changes that accompany old age and how old people may best cope with these changes, it focuses on *how old people maintain a sense of continuity and meaning that helps them cope with change.*

In my interviews with many old people who reflected on the course of their lives, I found that the ageless self maintains continuity through a symbolic, creative process. The self draws meaning from the past, interpreting and recreating it as a resource for being in the present. It also draws meaning from the structural and ideational aspects of the cultural context. Thus, I view the self as the interpreter of experience: from this perspective, individual identity is revealed by the patterns of symbolic meaning that characterize the individual's unique interpretation of experience.

Identity is not frozen in a static moment of the past. Old people formulate and reformulate personal and cultural symbols of their past to create a meaningful, coherent sense of self, and in the process they create a viable present. In this way, the ageless self emerges: its definition is ongoing, continuous, and creative.

Theoretical Foundations

The research for this book grew out of my work in two disciplines—cultural anthropology and social gerontology. Thus, my inquiry into identity and sources of meaning in old age is shaped largely by the theories and perspectives of these two fields.

Understanding the dynamic nature of the relationship between culture, that abstract word, and observable behavior in individual and group life has been the central issue in cultural anthropology since the discipline arose. In recent anthropological studies of old age and old people, this relationship has been widely investigated. Scholars have described and analyzed older people's behavior and their own interpretations of their lives in a variety of settings, from peasant and tribal villages to retirement residences in industrialized countries. The concept of *culture* is central to these investigations, even though anthropologists have never agreed upon its precise definition.[3]

The "classic," most pervasive definition of culture considers it the sum or aggregate of customs, traditions, and behaviors that are learned and shared among a group of people. Different aspects of custom and tradition have been emphasized by anthropologists. Some have looked at material artifacts, technology, ecology, or production. Others have focused upon institutions, social relations, religious beliefs, or ritual processes. In studies of old people, anthropologists have observed the impact of these customs and processes on the status, functioning, and treatment of elderly people within societies, communities, or particular ethnic groups.

Geertz (1973) and others have expanded this definition to emphasize the ideational dimension—culture is a set of shared understandings and symbols that characterize a group of people. "Culture consists of socially established structures of meaning . . ." (1973:12). In this view, culture provides an individual with a framework for making sense of and interpreting his or her own life and its larger contexts. This is the definition I employ in analyzing the lives of old people. I am investigating the shared understandings and symbols that affect old people, that are created by them, and that inform their accounts of their lives.

The study of culture from this perspective entails the ability to discern patterns in and make generalizations about the shared understandings and behavior of many individuals, be they members of one society or several. The cultural patterning of *individual* behavior has been a major concern to those anthropologists interested in the interface between psychological and sociocultural processes. Numerous studies of childrearing practices and adolescent behavior have focused on the processes by which an individual becomes *cultural* in the first place. Anthropologists have defined and clarified the role played by cultural norms and practices in personality formation and development. Their work, however, has focused only on the early years of life. They have not, by and large, addressed the issues of how culture continues to influence personality and behavior into old age, how identity is maintained when one is old, or how elderly individuals select and manipulate cultural goals and norms. This book investigates these issues.

Researchers in the field of social gerontology have studied the relationship between individual development and aging, but unlike anthropologists, they have not employed the concept of culture, however defined, in their studies. Gerontologists have turned to the discipline of developmental psychology for both theoretical inspiration and research techniques. The general concerns of this discipline—change and continuity studied within the context of the entire life span—have provided the basis for specific research questions in the area of personal development and aging. Buhler (1935, [Buhler and Massarik] 1968), Jung (1963), and Erikson (1959, 1963, 1968) have laid the theoretical groundwork for a psychology of aging and, more broadly, a psychology of the life cycle. But only Erikson, in his delineation of eight stages of the life cycle, offers researchers in aging a full-scale model for studying the dynamics of identity, continuity, and change throughout the entire life span. He formulates the process by which a person's identity grows and expands through the crises faced and choices made at different stages of development: basic trust vs. basic mistrust, autonomy vs. shame and doubt, initiative vs. guilt, industry vs. inferiority, identity vs. role confusion, intimacy vs. isolation, generativity vs. stagnation, and ego integrity vs. despair. Erikson's case study of Dr. Borg (1976) elaborates the last two stages—generativity vs. stagnation and ego integrity vs. despair—which are, according to his model, the major concerns of maturity and old age, respectively.

My research can be viewed in the context of Erikson's developmental model. In his scheme, the crisis of generativity concerns "establishing and guiding the next generation." It includes both productivity and creativity but is not limited to them alone. Ego integrity implies resolution of the issues inherent in the preceding seven stages. "It is the acceptance of one's one and only life cycle as something that had to be and that, by necessity, permitted of no substitutions" (Erikson 1963:263–269). My aim is to illustrate in detail the process by which individuals integrate and accept the diverse experiences of a lifetime, so that they achieve the final stage of development outlined by Erikson.

In both anthropology and gerontology, some key questions of change and continuity in adult development remain unanswered. Using both the concept of culture as an interpretive enterprise and the idea of identity development as a dynamic, ongoing process, my work offers new perspectives on four of these questions.

First, a subject of concern to social gerontologists has been the measurement of the passage of time in the individual life. A problem has been to choose appropriate frameworks of measurement—such as calendar time, social time, historical time—and to discover how they interact in the determination of behavior. There are few studies which report on the subjective experience of time to the elderly.[4] Through the analysis of subjective accounts of the entire life span, this book explores the meaning of different time periods and the meaning of the passage of time itself to the elderly.

A second issue is that of conceptual and methodological problems involved in the use of chronological age as a key variable in understanding the aging process. In recent years, researchers have found that variations in behavior are associated not with chronological age itself, but rather with other factors such as stressful events or cohort effects.[5] Indeed, Neugarten (1977:633, 1985) calls age an "empty variable," stressing that it is the biological and social events associated with the passage of time, and not merely time itself, which have relevance for the study of identity development. I would like to add that not only are the biological and social changes that occur with time relevant for the analysis of identity and aging, but more important, it is *the ways in which these events are interpreted by individuals in relation to the passage of time* that have a greater potential for explaining the process of change and continuity in late life.

Third, possibly the most important focus for gerontological research has been the relationship of personality to successful adaptation (also termed *morale* and *life satisfaction*). This area of interest gave rise to the major theories in social gerontology in the 1960s and continues to be of significant interest. A popular line of inquiry has been the role played by both change and continuity in adaptation. Neugarten (1968), Maddox (1968), and other researchers in the field of aging have proposed that continuity is a key to psychological well-being in old age. Their work and that of their colleagues analyzes continuity in terms of social activity only; it does not elaborate upon the meaning of continuity in the individual life, nor the part played by cultural values, norms, and expectations in the maintenance of continuity. More recently, studies in psychology and life-span development are exploring the relationship between change and continuity in the individual life and how this relationship is subjectively perceived. Current research addressing this relationship proposes that both change and continuity characterize normal development *throughout* the entire life span (Brim and Kagan 1980; Featherman 1983). The ways in which the individual responds to both the impact of change and the enduring features of the aging process will influence the structure of the life course and the individual's interpretation of it (Cohler 1982; Ryff 1984).

Fourth, a body of theory that contrasts with developmental psychology but which is used as a framework of orientation by a growing number of researchers in the fields of both anthropology and gerontology is symbolic interactionism. Students of this school of thought, originating with George Herbert Mead, point out that people are not passive observers and reactors to their surroundings; rather they actively participate in their environment, creating their social reality and sense of self as they engage in community life and as they interpret and evaluate the meaning of their interactions with others. The self-concept grows and changes as one continues to interpret one's environment and interactions throughout life.

Interactionists who have studied aging have emphasized change in adulthood. They view change as the outcome of socialization and situational adjustment, two processes believed to continue throughout the life span. When considered along with developmental studies, this approach adds considerably to our knowledge of adult development in a social context. Yet, interactionists have not fully confronted the issues of consistency and continuity in the elderly person's life. Some unanswered questions remain. If one's self-concept is a product of social interaction, how can one preserve a coherent sense of self throughout the life course as the interactions change? How does one maintain a sense of self that integrates 70 years or more of diverse experience, a lifetime of communication with a variety of people, and participation in different kinds of events? I have found that in the expression of the ageless self, individuals not only symbolically preserve and integrate meaningful components of their pasts, but they also use these symbols as frameworks for understanding and being in the present.

Methods and Themes

The following pages explore the concept of the ageless self as it was expressed in interviews with 60 urban, white, middle-class Californians over the age of 70. I selected individuals whom I had met over a two-year period during visits to nursing homes, retirement residences, senior centers, retiree support groups, and through personal and professional referrals. For nine months in 1978 and 1979, I met with them on a one-to-one basis for conversations and observed and participated with some of them in their daily rounds, with friends and family, in routine situations, and during periods of celebration, crisis, anxiety, and contentment. Although some were not in good health, all 60 people were mentally alert and articulate. I deliberately chose alert, expressive individuals for this project, knowing that I would be talking with them extensively. I spent at least several hours with each of them during the fieldwork period, talking with them about their past life experiences, current family and social patterns, daily routines, and self-concepts. Thus my research centered on the individual life, its social and cultural context, how each person recalls and interprets experience, and the meaning that experience has for him or her.

The study group represents a variety of economic, occupational, and educational backgrounds, as well as current home environments. The 60 individuals do not reside in the same geographic community (though they all live in the same large metropolitan area), nor do they share identical lifestyles. Because the study group is not spatially bound, isolated, or identifiable, it cannot be described in terms of such social structural properties as community organization, politics, local institutions, networks, occupational roles, or other constructs common to urban or sociological studies. However, its members do share some cultural characteristics that provide a context for identity development: they have all been exposed to the same major social trends and national historic events in the United States over a period of approximately 50 years, and they share certain dominant American goals, values, and expectations.

From the initial 60, I chose a subsample of 15 people for intensive, systematic interviewing to elicit their life stories in some detail. These 15 typify the range of past and present experience of the larger group.

Although the terms *life history* and *life story* generally have been used interchangeably in anthropology, in this book I follow the sociologist Bertaux's distinction between the terms. He uses *life stories* to mean "accounts of a person's life as delivered orally by the person himself" (1981 : 7–8). In contrast, a *life history* is a personal account supplemented by biographical information drawn from other sources (such as official records, interviews with other people, or letters) so that "truthfulness" can be checked. In these terms, I collected life stories.*

I collected life stories in order to study the relationships among old age, personal reflection, and identity. I told my informants I wanted to learn about their lives in order to understand these issues better. I gathered life stories in the

---

* Bertaux (1981 : 5–11) makes a further distinction between life story and life history on the one hand—both of which focus on the *oral* account, created in collaboration with the researcher—and autobiography and biography on the other hand. These latter terms refer to well-established *literary* forms. Anthropologists have not adhered to such distinctions and, indeed, have used all four terms to refer to a variety of aspects of collection, analysis, or presentation of personal, oral accounts of a life. Indeed, anthropologists have added to the terminological—and thus methodological—confusion by also using the term *case history* and by inventing the phrase "anthropological biography" (Crapanzano 1984).

context of discursive conversations that dealt with everyday life, events, and concerns. I did not gather chronological life histories in order to present them as such or to illustrate an aspect of urban, middle-class American culture.[6] Rather, I collected life stories to explore the issue of continuity and meaning in old age. I was interested in what elements from the past would appear in life story interviews, and how these elements would be expressed.

The life story interviews I conducted ranged from 8 to 15 hours in length, divided into two, three, or four sessions. These were tape-recorded, and the tapes were later fully transcribed. In addition to the life stories, I recorded many conversations with members of the subsample, covering a range of subjects from the abstractions of their philosophies of life to the concreteness of mundane, daily tasks.

The interviews were not conducted with a view toward preserving a life story for posterity; I was not recording "oral history." People did not relate the story of their lives to me in a premeditated, planned, or organized manner. I saw no evidence that they were trying to present a unified account or a one-sided, glamorous view of themselves. Also, people did not talk about their lives in relation to social trends or the times in which they have lived. They did not place themselves in a broader historical context.

All conversations and interviews, tape-recorded or not, were informal in style. Though I never used a precise pre-worded questionnaire, I did follow an interview guide (see Appendix) and asked each informant the same questions, though not necessarily in the same order. My questions were designed to get people to talk about what was meaningful to them, rather than to have specific queries answered. To have followed a detailed questionnaire would have forced people to structure their answers according to the researcher's priorities rather than their own. In gathering life stories, I wanted to learn what details they would include as pertinent. My guiding principle was to ask questions that would get people to talk about (1) what was meaningful in their pasts, and (2) how they describe themselves now in old age.

I explained to everyone involved in this research that I am an anthropologist interested in aging and that I wanted to learn something about their pasts, what they think have been the important experiences in life, how they describe themselves, how they feel about growing older, and what have been their frustrations, successes, and hopes. I told them that I hope my findings will contribute to our knowledge of the aging process. No informant was paid to participate in the research.

I tried to place my informants in the role of teacher. I think I was most often put in the role of empathetic acquaintance. For a number of people, I was a confidant. From my viewpoint, and I think from that of my informants as well, our conversations were undertaken in a spirit of friendliness, honesty, and enjoyment. Data that I obtained in this manner were spontaneous, thoughtful, and usually self-reflective. Anyone overhearing one of my "interviews" (except another anthropologist) probably would have thought that we were friends carrying on a conversation, or that we were acquaintances, and that I was simply trying to get to know the other person better. This is the context in which I acquired information about identity.

Material I collected was anchored in the occurrences of everyday life and the individual's immediate environment. The life stories were created from accumulated memories and judgments about past and present circumstances within the framework of informants' perceptions of and reactions to me and my general interests.

I chose a life story approach for studying the process of self-formulation in old age for several reasons. First, the life story reveals subjective experience; it is the individual's view of how he or she understands his or her own life (Watson

1976). Second, because lives are lived in a cultural context, the life story is constructed from that context, allowing us to see how cultural sources are employed in the formulation of identity. Third, through life stories, people "account"[7] for their lives, that is, they make them logical and coherent and imbue them with a sense of naturalness and rightness. They select, define, classify, and organize experience in order to express the reality of their lives and permeate that reality with meaning.

Both anthropologists and gerontologists have noted the problems of reliability and validity inherent in such a subjective and retrospective approach and the lack of a coherent, all-encompassing methodology with which to deal with these problems.[8] In studying identity in old age, external measures of validity are not critical if one is concerned with eliciting informants' *current interpretations* of their lives— what they view as the relevant sequence and timing of events, what they perceive to have been meaningful experiences, and the way in which they now understand their relationship to other individuals and institutions over time.

Chronological age has little usefulness in explaining individual differences or in building theory in gerontology. Researchers from different disciplines suggest that "process" variables have more explanatory power than do demographic variables for interpreting the meaning and complexities of the aging process.[9] In my analysis of life stories, I have concentrated on a specific "process" variable or construct which I have called a *theme.* *

---

* Morris Opler (1945:198) uses the word *theme* in his discussion of world view and values: "a postulate or position, declared or implied, and usually controlling behavior or stimulating activity which is tacitly approved or openly promoted in a society . . ." I am using the word differently here. I use the term in its English language usage: "a topic or subject" (*Webster's New World Dictionary*, 1966). In the context of my research, the term *theme* refers to a component part of a self. These component parts emerged as people told me their life stories.

The concept of theme emerged after I collected, and then studied, several life stories. No informant self-consciously described to me the themes in his or her life, nor were themes set forth in any organized manner as the life stories were told. Yet, though they are not deliberately fashioned, the themes people create are the means by which they interpret and evaluate their life experiences and attempt to integrate these experiences to form a self-concept.

In the description of their lives, people create *themes*—cognitive areas of meaning with symbolic force—which explain, unify, and give substance to their perceptions of who they are and how they see themselves participating in social life. As each life is unique, so too are the themes. But all themes have their sources in the historical, geographical, and social circumstances in which people live, the flow of ordinary daily life, the values of American society, and cultural expectations of how a life should be lived. Thus, themes are informed by shared as well as individual experience. As people interpret the events, experiences, conditions, and priorities of their lives—making connections and drawing conclusions as they proceed—they formulate themes. In this way, individuals know themselves and explain who they are to others.

The following examples illustrate components of themes expressed by informants who participated in the research upon which this book is based: "My entire life has been devoted to my law practice"; "My family is my life—I am nothing without them"; and "I spent many years serving the community. I would say that the best way to live a good life is to do as much as you can for others." Themes are organizational and explanatory markers that emerge as individuals relate their life stories. Though jobs, social activities, friendship patterns, family relations, living arrangements, and health status may change over the years, individuals, through the expression of themes, are able to connect and integrate the diverse experiences of a lifetime. In this way, continuity is created and maintained symbolically in the individual life.

In the case studies which follow, I have restructured, edited, and re-presented the life stories by theme to illustrate how individuals formulate an identity in the process of reflecting upon, evaluating, and describing their lives. The self-formulations are not based on chronological age. I found as well that old people do not define themselves directly through a chronology of life experiences. Rather, they define themselves through the expression of selected life experiences. They do not identify themselves by concepts of the past or historical moments in which they have lived. Nor do they view their lives solely, or predominantly, in terms of roles played, however significant certain roles have been. Rather, people crystalize certain experiences into *themes.* Thus themes, as reformulated experience, can be considered building blocks of identity. Identity in old age—the ageless self—is founded on the present significance of past experience, the current rendering of meaningful symbols and events of a life.

To present and explore themes that emerge from life stories, I have organized the following pages around three broad questions: What themes are expressed as people in this study group tell their life stories? What are the sources of themes— where do they come from? And how do themes operate in shaping identity? First, I will focus upon themes as they emerged from the life stories of three individuals. Then, I will broaden the perspective to look at themes in terms of their cultural sources. There is no single explanation for the emergence of themes and, thus, the expression of an identity, just as there is no single explanation for the existence and sequence of particular events in a life. People formulate at least several themes when describing their lives. And, as I will show, themes have multiple sources. My intent is to illustrate how people create themes from their pasts, drawing meaning from (1) the choices they have made and limitations and opportunities they have faced because of social and historical conditions; and (2) the cultural values they have incorporated. Then, I will show how themes integrate experience in meaningful ways to meet two challenges of identity formulation in late life: providing a sense of continuity across the life span, and reconciling the course of a life with ideals and expectations of how a life should be lived.

Two

Themes in the Life Story

I'd enjoy talking with you but I feel a bit guilty and
hypocritical. Between the things I've forgotten, the things
I've repressed, and the things I will not discuss, there's
not much left.

91-YEAR-OLD WOMAN

How do themes emerge from the life story? In my analysis of the 15 interviews, I treated the life stories as literary texts to be penetrated[1] rather than as supplementary
data to larger cultural configurations or illustrative material
in the study of a social group. Thus I scrutinized them in
great detail, looking for the nature of their uniqueness. I derived the themes from several readings of each verbatim
transcript of the tape-recorded life story interviews. Working
within the texts, I noted and coded repetition of specific
words, use of language and general thought patterns, the
structure of the overall life story, and the subject matter
which dominated the accounts as well as that which rarely
or never arose in discussion.[2]

In order to draw out integrative concepts in the texts, I

28

used specific techniques of the "grounded theory" approach of Glaser and Strauss (1967; [Glaser] 1978) to develop what they refer to as "substantive codes." When studying the transcribed interviews, I asked: What is this data about? And, what does this data tell me about how the person conceives his or her own life? I then analyzed the data line by line, coding each sentence. Focusing on patterns of organization in the transcribed texts and repetition of words or phrases, I generated "substantive codes," which "conceptualize the empirical substance of the area of research" (Glaser 1978:55–57).*

First, I generated many substantive codes for each life story (there were about 15–20 for each story). These codes were words or phrases that an informant used repeatedly such as "like," "love," and "became attached." Then, I grouped most of the codes into categories and gave each category a name. For example, I grouped "like," "love," and "became attached" together on the basis of their interchangeable usage in the life story. I named this category of codes *affective ties.* All codes were grouped into categories on the basis of their similarity of meaning in the context of the story. Four to six categories were created for each life story. These categories of substantive codes I have called *themes.*[3] They represent conceptions of meaning that emerge over and over in the texts. Only codes that appear many times have been grouped into categories and designated as themes. Repetition of words and phrases has both explanatory and integrative power: themes emerge from a text as symbolic signposts, defining a particular framework of understanding. In addition, themes are symbolically connected to one another by various threads

---

*Glaser and Strauss (1967) and Glaser (1978) note that the analyst must do his or her own coding. A hired coder needs a list of codes; there are no preconceived codes with the grounded theory approach. This approach is inductive and intuitive; it stimulates codes or ideas and is an interpretive and creative endeavor.

in the story to create a cohesive and coherent retrospective account.

I have described themes by topics (marriage, work, religion) or by interpretive labels (self-determination, acquiescence, disengagement). The two types of themes do not indicate distinct methodological or theoretical approaches. Both types refer to the categorization of codes that have explanatory power and symbolic force for the individual. The different labels for these themes reflect the different sources of meaning individuals draw upon in formulating identity. Topics represent social structural features or properties that have symbolic meaning for the person; interpretive labels reflect the individual's sense of self in the world—the identification with certain cultural norms, goals, or expectations, and the evaluation of personal behavior.

The life story interviews took place over a period of several months. During this time, I gathered additional information by participant-observation. By visiting with informants in their homes, as well as interviewing them, I was able to observe their behavior in ordinary, daily life and participate with them in routine activities. I applied this data to my analysis in the following ways: First, I used it descriptively to characterize the individuals who are portrayed in the pages that follow. Second, I used participant-observation data to test themes I identified from the life stories against behavior I observed—informants' behavior corroborated certain themes. Finally, I used this data to illustrate how themes are expressed in current behavior.

In identifying themes, I analyzed the life stories along three dimensions—content, timing, and style[4]—three aspects of the life story that reveal the individual's sense of self in the world. *Content* is established by each informant as he or she places emphasis and value on particular events, relationships, institutions, and ideas. One informant stated: "I was ambitious—a doer. I'm still a doer. I've never gotten out of wanting to be doing work all the time. I believe it's your God-given duty to do something, to accomplish something." This man's action-orientation and sense of ambition permeate his entire life story.

Timing is revealed by the way the individual organizes his or her past. As we shall see, one woman told me, "I had three husbands; I had three completely different lifestyles." The notion of one's own life course, occurring in time, includes concepts of sequence, the flow of events, and causality. People structure their accounts by utilizing time markers that reflect their own interpretation of their pasts. Contrary to the popular notion of the life course as a trajectory, timing as revealed in the life story is highly idiosyncratic. As the story unfolds, an individual divides and arranges experience into coherent bits and pieces so that phases of the life span, turning points, and high points emerge according to how the individual conceives his or her own experience.

Because they are articulated in the presence of another human being, life stories have a *style*. I use *style* here, first of all, in Erving Goffman's (1974:288) sense of the word: "the maintenance of expressive identifiability." An individual will tell his or her life story, or engage in any other social activity, in a particular and singular manner which the listener or observer interprets as being an indication of the individual's "core" or "central" self. Style also entails "impression management" (Goffman 1959)—sustaining a certain image of oneself in a given situation or series of situations. The storyteller will reveal only some information to the listener and only parts of his or her self. Other interpretations and assessments will be withheld. Thus style is the *expressive* manifestation of identity. Through the presentation of a particular style, a person maintains his or her identifiability in the world.

Style includes self-evaluation. As one articulates an identity, one expresses one's notion of self-worth and performance in the larger world. One woman expressed style in the following comment: "I wasted so many years because I was shy and scared. I was too afraid to do things. I refused that job because I lacked self-confidence." In the case studies that follow, I have examined these three dimensions of self-expression in the life story to illustrate how individuals symbolically interpret their experience to formulate a coherent sense of identity in old age.

I have picked three stories from the sample of 15 interviews to illustrate a variety of attitudes, personal experiences, current activities, and lifestyles. The range of themes in the 15 cases is broad; in addition, the themes are not, in most cases, directly comparable. The three life stories I have chosen to present are exceptional only in that they have the most content and richness of the 15 I collected. They do not contain more themes than any of the other stories: I elicited four to six major themes from each person's life story.

Because detailed life stories and their emergent themes are unique and idiosyncratic, one cannot speak of a "typical" life or a "typical" set of themes. These three particular lives were chosen to convey the range of personal experience and cultural background among study participants. They are not more or less typical of the subsample or entire study group than are any other lives. And, they are not necessarily more remarkable or dramatic.

Millie[5]

Millie is 80 years old. She had been living in a nursing home for about a year before I met her—long enough to recover from the trauma of being institutionalized, to feel comfortable with the routine and personnel of the place, to make some decisions about how she would deal with her new life, and to act on these decisions. The first time I walked into the Home and stood in the doorway surveying the large lounge area, she spotted me, said: "Hello. Who are you? What are you doing here?" and proceeded to chat with me easily about various things. I soon realized that she is one of the most friendly, outgoing, and lively people in this large facility. Her eyes shine with enthusiasm for life, and she is quick to laugh. These features make her an attractive-looking woman. Though she looks hardy and robust, she is rather unsteady physically, walks laboriously with a cane, struggles to sit and stand, and needs help when dressing and bathing. She hardly ever discusses her infirmities, ignores the limitations they place upon her, and is as active as she can be.

Affective ties is the essential theme Millie employed in explaining herself and her life to me. Discussions of the quality and quantity of affective ties are the most meaningful way for her to describe who she is, how she has gotten along in the world throughout her life, and how she understands events that take place around her. Most of our conversations over an eight-month period centered around her relationships with people both in her past and at the present time.

All the people who come into her life are viewed in terms of the emotional connection they have with her. She "likes" or "dislikes," "is attracted to," "cares for," or "loves" everyone with whom she comes into contact. A strong need for affection dominates her interactions and her thinking process, and she is fully aware of this. She uses the word *attach* repeatedly. "I grew very attached to him and he to me"; "We developed an attachment for one another"; "I am so attached to her." *Love* is another frequently used word in her vocabulary. "I love her and she loves me" and "We love one another" are phrases she uses often.

She divides people into two groups, based on the type of emotional commitment others convey to her. There are "family," those whose love and caring she can count on, and then there are "strangers," those whose affective attachment to herself is not reliable or long-lasting. The qualities in people that are important to her are those that family members are supposed to have, such as loyalty, sincerity, attentiveness. Millie measures the worth of all relationships in terms of these qualities. She wants and needs all people with whom she comes into contact, regardless of role, to have these qualities, and she is very disappointed when she finds out that this is not the case. In addition, she expects everyone in her world to have an emotional commitment to her and to think about her.

The people with whom she interacts most frequently now are the nurses, aides, volunteers, and other residents in the institution, and she talks about them in terms of whether or not and how much they care for her and are "attached" to her. She expects each interaction to be of a loving character. When an aide hurriedly hands her the breakfast tray and says nothing, Millie feels betrayed. As far as she is concerned, the aide is not treating her as she should, that is, with love, respect, and devotion. When she meets someone at the Home and develops a nodding acquaintance, she speaks of "liking" that person (for instance, a volunteer or the man who delivers the mail). After a brief time, this "liking" generally becomes "being attached." She creates a pattern of interpersonal relations in which a positive response to someone new in her life is turned into a relationship of reciprocal emotional commitment. She thus sets herself up for frequent disappointment.

From her earliest childhood memories, nothing stands out so importantly as the need to develop, maintain, and express close, emotional ties. "My mother cherished me"; "I adored my father and he clung to me"; "I adored my principal. I'll never forget him"; "I was attached to the other children in the neighborhood. . . . I took care of all of them." Later, "I loved my piano teacher and felt so close to her." Her life story does not contain many descriptions of the character traits of others. She sees other people primarily in terms of their affective relationship with herself.

Indeed, she often explains other people's behavior in terms of whether or not and to what extent they are close to her. For example, "My daughter left me" states the relevant aspect of this child's move to another city. Millie interprets this as a personal loss; by moving, the daughter temporarily severed her end of the emotional commitment. And then, "My son is moving out here to be near me." This is the only causal reason Millie gives for this act, though she has discussed his job change and other particulars about the move. Its significance to her clearly lies in the personal gain it represents.

Millie's characterization of people by their ties to her finds its most extreme expression in the way she describes her current best friend. In Millie's descriptions of K., K. has no independent character traits at all. She is represented as existing only in relation to Millie, as tied to her, not as an autonomous human being. This is not to say that if pressed, Millie would be unable to describe K. as a person, but that Millie's "uncritical attitude" (Watson 1976:120) stresses the ties rather than the individual personalities in her world. When I first asked Millie about K., she stated: "Without me, she's lost. I put her in her place; I bawl her out. . . . K. is true-blue. E. tried to take her away from me, but she wouldn't sit by E. unless I sat with her." In Millie's perception, K. is an extension of Millie; Millie tells her what to do and knows that K. would not act without Millie's approval.

Besides describing other people in terms of their bond with her, Millie describes herself only in relation to other people—in terms of the quality of her feelings about the people she knows, and in terms of her perceptions of others' feelings toward her. When I asked her to describe herself now, she pondered for a few minutes and then replied: "I love them all here, I love the way they feel about me, the attention. I know it's real and sincere, and I'm sincere. I'm a very lovable and affectionate person."

In the Home now, Millie creates a world in which—at least

in form—emotional commitments abound. For example, when she meets someone walking down the hall, she frequently stops and says: "Hello, darling. How are you today? How did you sleep last night? I love you." This often elicits the response, "I'm fine thank you; I love you too." At this, Millie smiles, is obviously pleased with the encounter, and walks on. Many times she has introduced me to an aide, saying, "Sharon, I'd like you to meet ———; we've become very attached to one another, haven't we?" And the aide can only respond, "Yes, we have." Millie sets up these interactions in a way that affirms her sense of self as a lovable person.

She engages in other behavior which affirms the lovable self as well. A roommate with whom Millie was getting along badly mentioned that she tore her skirt. Millie offered to mend it. According to Millie, after it was repaired the roommate replied: "You're the dearest person I know. I adore you. I love you. Please don't leave me." Millie was needed, and their relationship improved for a time after this episode. Millie frequently assists people with canes or wheelchairs to and from the dining room. On occasions when I have been there, the person helped has not said merely "Thank you," but "Millie, you're the most unselfish person I've ever met," and "Millie you're so thoughtful, and with all your troubles too." Before moving to the Home, she was hospitalized for several months. Of that time she says: "While I was in the hospital I also was considered a helper. I helped whoever I could. The doctor considered me one of the most outstanding patients, in improving and in helping." Thus, her behavior is infused with expectations of mutual respect and loving responses from others. By giving help openly and joyously when she thinks it is needed, Millie elicits affectionate responses from others. Moreover, she portrays social interaction as a competition: she wants to be the best at what she does—gathering affection. We can begin to understand the emphasis she places on affective ties, and one of the possible reasons for it, when we look at the way she tells her life story, for this shows us how she draws meaning from her life experiences.

Though Millie characterizes her early relationship with her parents in terms of strong affective ties, her description of her childhood emphasizes emotional deprivation: she apparently did not receive the love and attention she needed, and her relationships with family members were not stable or gratifying. The way she describes her early years now imparts a Cinderella quality to her childhood: she was the poor, unfortunate one, pushed around and neglected by other family members.

She was born in Brooklyn, in 1898, of German-Jewish immigrant parents, 1 of 10 or 12 children. She is not sure of the exact number because some of her siblings died in infancy. She was one of the youngest and was the second daughter. She has always compared herself unfavorably with her older sister, the lucky, favored one in the family. "S. was a prima donna. So beautiful and talented. She was an artist and a singer. I was the domesticated one. I helped my mother with all the housework. . . . My sister was studying for operatic stage." From her earliest childhood, Millie has envied this sister for the attention she received from their mother and her chance to pursue a career which led, according to Millie, to prestige and wealth. Millie dwells on the fact that her own childhood opportunities were severely limited because her mother did not pay as much attention to her.

Millie's father was not around much, and she says that she did not receive the affection she needed from him either. Her childhood memories of her father are sparse. "I remember how unhappy mother was because he was a card player, and out late at night. He didn't help raise the family. It was all for my mother to do, and there was a lot of worry." She did not receive much personal attention from her brothers, who were much older than she. Some were out working, and others had moved away by the time she was a small child.

Financial insecurity is part of Millie's story as well. Millie's father was in and out of real estate ventures, and he was not an entirely successful breadwinner. Millie's older brothers contributed to the financially precarious household and seem to have kept the family solvent during her childhood. When she was 16, Millie had to quit school and go to work to support herself and contribute to the household. She had taken commercial courses—typing, stenography, bookkeeping—in school, and she got a job as a bookkeeper in a jewelry store. There, she met her first husband and married at the age of 17.

The timing dimension of Millie's story centers on *marriage,* a second theme in her story. In the course of our discussions, I asked her, "If you were writing the story of your life, how would you divide it into chapters?" She answered: "Well, I had three husbands"; and later, "I had three completely different lifestyles." Millie's three marriages appear in her story as the major turning points in her life, transitions to which she had to adapt by restructuring her lifestyle. The setting of priorities in her life and the organization of her experience evolved in response to her relationships with her three husbands. But though her relationships with all three men were different and demanded from her different roles, she made the necessary adjustments to them while maintaining and affirming important aspects of her identity.

Millie looks back on her first marriage as a storybook romance. She adored her husband; he adored her. "I became a very wealthy woman, and very happy. I had three children. I had a beautiful life." She blossomed as a mother, homemaker, and business partner to her husband. This emerges as the high point in her life. She never again describes herself as happy without reservation. This is the only man in her life she considers her "real" husband, the person with whom she had a perfect relationship. When I asked her what periods in her life stand out vividly, she replied, "When I lost my husband, naturally." He died after they had been married for 15 years.

She had worked with him in the jewelry business, and when he died, she continued to work. She regards this experience as a success. "I got a job in the jewelry business, and after awhile, I understood diamonds better than some men, even today. I even repaired watches." *Work* quickly became for her the most meaningful way to enhance her self-esteem. It emerges as the third theme in her story. Only through work did she feel capable and worthwhile in the social world. In fact, she states that her biggest success in life was her continual employment. "I was in demand," she told me, "I was always pulled from one position to another"; and "I was always capable of getting good jobs. . . . In no time I picked up the business." She adapted easily to the numerous and varied jobs she held throughout her life and is very proud of this fact. One reason she views her ability to adapt in this sphere as a major success is that it counters the difficulty she had contending with both the lifestyles her second and third husbands imposed upon her and the transition periods between marriages. Her jobs were also critical to her emotional well-being. First, they were a way to ease the pain of the death of her first husband. "I had to work . . . but I worked also to relieve my mind and try to forget my husband." Later, work gave her emotional strength and specific purpose during her subsequent marriages.

In telling her life story, she does not describe the specific nature of the jobs she held from the time her first marriage ended until she stopped working at age 67. Rather, as with her social interactions, Millie describes her employment history in terms of competition. "I answered this ad in the paper. I went to see this man who had a jewelry store. And he said to me, 'You know what? I've interviewed 40 or 50 people, and I want you for the job.'" And later: "I went into this beautiful store of ladies' clothes. There was a sign in the window, Lady Wanted. All I knew about clothes was what I wore. The man accepted me; there were eight other girls on that floor. Before you knew it, in no time, I was making more sales than all of them. . . ." Through competition in work, Millie is able to view herself as a success in the world and, perhaps more important, to emphasize some positive aspects of her experience to balance the traumas and disappointment in her second and third marriages.

Millie describes these marriages as utterly unfulfilling. She portrays her second husband as "brilliant," "talented," and "useful," but nowhere in describing their relationship does she use any word except *stormy* in denoting affect. She never denigrates his character. He was a furniture designer, 20 years her senior, and according to Millie, he wanted her to be a "constant companion" on business trips and to accompany him to the theater and concerts. He was very well-to-do; Millie married him to relieve her financial struggles. She described to me in detail the beautiful home and furniture he bought her.

When they were first married, he told her then-teenage children he could not live with them—they cramped his style. So they moved away, an event which devastated Millie. After several years, she became pregnant. "You see, I wasn't supposed to get pregnant at all. . . . He was very annoyed and wanted me to do away with the baby." She entered this marriage on his terms, and by having a baby, she broke the contract. After the child was born, her husband abused her and the marriage deteriorated. To make matters worse, Millie could not develop a satisfying relationship with his child. "I couldn't get her to love me. I couldn't. And I tried every which way." This period was extremely trying for a woman who needed much affection and was getting none. She says of this time: "The baby was in his way. The baby is what kept me going. . . . That baby was my life, kept me as happy as I was able to be." This marriage ended in divorce after about five years, an experience that filled Millie with shame.

Five years later, at 45, Millie remarried. She describes her third husband as a "poor little fella. . . . I had no attachment whatsoever to him." She says she married him for financial security and companionship. He was 10 years younger than she and "looked the picture of health. I didn't know he was a sick man." For the 25 years they were married, he was in and out of hospitals with various illnesses, and Millie nursed him at home quite a bit. They moved around the country several times, seeking a better climate for him. She talks about these years in terms of the geographic moves they made, the apartments they fixed up, and the disagreements they had with other tenants and landlords. Her husband figures in these discussions as another object to be considered in the move to a new place—something else to look after.

She spent more years financially supporting their marriage than did her husband. During this phase of her life, her work not only provided their income, but kept her from dwelling on her frustrations and from getting depressed. "I couldn't take staying at home"; "Sitting drove me crazy"; "I needed to do something"—are ways in which she describes her situation when she was between jobs. During this marriage she managed apartment buildings and held numerous clerical and retail jobs. This husband died when she was 70, 10 years before I met her.

In Millie's story her second husband's volatile personality and impossible demands created an emotionally pressured situation from which she barely survived intact mentally. The third husband turned out to be neither financially secure nor a companion. She speaks of these marriages—much of her life—as "hardships" that she "managed to endure," and as "a very trying existence." Certainly she does not depict either marriage as providing the intimacy she craves. Her second and third husbands are the only people she never describes in terms of affective ties!

Several themes have emerged from Millie's life story so far. *Affective ties* provide the central meaning in her experience. The *marriages* are the structure upon which she builds her life story. She defines her social worth and success through *work*. A fourth theme that emerges from her story is an emphasis on *social status*. She describes people by their status only, not by their character traits. For example, newcomers to the Home are categorized as "brilliant" or "rich." Acquaintances are seen as "rich," "beautiful," or "having a magnificent home." Family members are variously described as "prominent," "outstanding," "wealthy," and "not rich, but brilliant."

The social status of others has special meaning for her. She has always valued material wealth and personal accomplishment, and though she cannot demonstrate achievement in these areas through many of her own activities, she has nevertheless devised a way to acquire status—by means of association. She creates a world in which she is surrounded by successful others. She does not measure herself against the status of others, nor absorb the success of those with whom she interacts, but she is able to reach some level of satisfaction knowing that people in her world have achieved what she values. Thus the sister Millie envied as a child and feels close to now is presently described as a "prominent, successful artist. She married very well, had a 13-room house, was left well-off as a widow . . . and she's gorgeous." Her sister's affluence and achievements are Millie's vicarious link to a more glamorous life, a life she has craved but been unable to make her own.

Only at one point in her life did Millie attain a sense of personal achievement and social status—when she studied music as a teenager. Looking back, she feels this was the most influential experience of her life.

One of my girlfriends was quite well-to-do. She was taking piano lessons, and my family couldn't afford it. My oldest brother was like a father then, and I went crying to him that I wanted to study the piano. So, he let me. I went to this woman's home and took lessons from her. I'll never forget it. It was about a mile away, and I walked there every day to practice for over a year because I had no piano and I had to wait until my brother could afford to buy me one. I went every day. And I felt so proud, carrying my valise, with my music rolled up, walking back and forth. And he finally bought me a piano. I think it was in the $200 bracket. And I was the happiest child in the world. I stayed three or four years, long enough to be able to teach. . . .

This incident is highly charged for Millie. For one thing, studying music put her in the same league with her talented older sister. Her own talent and artistic worth were finally acknowledged. Piano lessons also gave her status in the community. Only middle-class children studied music; her lessons made her feel like one of them. Carrying her valise in public to and from her lessons made her into a member of the community with status. With her music under her arm she was a special person, talented and well-off, and recognized as such.

This is the only episode in the account of her life in which she is proud of herself. She does not use that word, or any equivalent, again, for there have been no subsequent incidents in her life which elicited pride. Pride in one's achievements, however defined, is a critical component of self-worth in American society. With no feeling of material or artistic achievement since her teenage years, it is no wonder that Millie creates a way to acquire status by association now.

When discussing her past, Millie's style—the manner in which she portrays herself to the world and sees herself interacting with others—is acquiescent; that is, she describes situations so that responsibility for her acts and decisions falls on others. The theme of *acquiescence* has two components: first, other people make decisions for Millie at critical life junctures; second, things happen to her that seem to be out of her hands. Millie explains the turns of events with a sense of fate, of external forces playing upon her, rather than of personal choice-making or autonomy.

In her life story Millie repeatedly acquiesces in decisions made by others, especially members of her family. When her second marriage became difficult and her husband asked her children to leave, they told her to stay with him and she complied, though that decision certainly did not resolve any problems for her. When the marriage became intolerable, she divorced because her doctor "ordered" her to do so. Then, the doctor "ordered me out of New Jersey with my baby. He said, 'This climate is not good for your child. Go to a warm climate.'" And she did. These changes, all major upheavals in her life, are interpreted by Millie to mean she had no part in making them come to pass. Perhaps she could not—and cannot still—take full responsibility for these actions, which were highly stressful at the time and did not by any means improve her situation.

She stated to me again and again that she had no intention of marrying a third time, not after such a traumatic second marriage. With a baby and a job, she felt she had her hands full and did not "want to look at a man." But then "circumstances led to it." The third husband followed her when she moved to another city, met her relatives, and convinced them to talk her into marrying him. She says:

> My brother and sister-in-law liked him very much.
> They got him in a room, and they talked it over. Then
> they said to me, "He is going to be a father to your
> child. He loves you. You'll have security." And they
> talked to me and talked to me. And I married him.

She was convinced or coerced into this marriage as she tells it, and she presents this act as being out of her hands and beyond her control.

When Millie discovered that her husband was seriously ill, her brother told her to take him to a doctor, and the doctor told her to move with him to a drier climate. "I listened to him. . . . I didn't like it, but I felt it was the best for him so I made the best of it." Apparently, the climate didn't help her husband, and the next thing to happen was that one of her children suggested she move to the West Coast. "We listened to her and sold everything."

She arrived and found an apartment but, "My daughter wouldn't let me live there." Shortly after she settled in an apartment that was approved by family members, her husband died. Millie describes the ensuing events as follows: "My son insisted I go to my brother and sister-in-law. They took care of me for a while. When I came back, the kids made me get out of the house." Her children "decided" she should move again, first to a retirement residence, then to the institution where she now resides. They also "pulled" her to the hospital when she was ill. These moves were not always to her liking, and occasionally she offered some resistance. But she always went along with them.

Acquiescence emerges as Millie describes her employment history also. She stated on different occasions: "I was *called* from one job to another"; "I was *taken* from one concern to another"; "I was *kidnapped* from one place to another." She describes each new job situation as happening by chance. For instance, she "accidentally" met someone who hired her, and later: "I don't know how it happened, but I got that job"; or "He hired me on account of my handwriting." It is ironic that Millie developed a sense of personal and social worth and now derives a large part of her self-esteem from her work history, yet she describes her job opportunities largely in terms of chance rather than skill.

Moving to the nursing facility where I met her was the most recent major transition in Millie's life. As with all her other upheavals, she has had to develop a way to cope with this one. She describes her arrival there: "I just wandered around. I had to really make my own way. And I don't know how I managed it, but I did. . . . I made up my mind to slowly and gradually manage it." From this point on Millie ceases to use passive verbs, and no longer portrays herself as compliant. Instead, she has started to speak of taking her life in her own hands and making decisions about how she will live.

A new theme emerges from her story when she discusses this current life phase: *self-determination*. This sixth theme represents Millie's decision to present herself to the world as in command of her situation. She told me that only in this way can she prevent herself from becoming overwhelmed and depressed by the institution.

In keeping with the importance she places on emotional commitment, Millie structures her relationships with purpose. As noted earlier, her best friend does what Millie wants and is who Millie needs her to be. And Millie manipulates general conversation so that she is sure of receiving verbal affection. When aides or other residents are not behaving toward her as she expects, she says: "I don't have to take that. You're here to respect me"; or "I don't have to take this language from you or anyone else. I love everyone and everyone here loves me." In this way, she perceptually "corrects" the substance of the interaction to redefine the nature of the relationship and, thus, heal her wounded self-esteem.

Millie has also assumed control over the daily rounds in the facility, a difficult thing to do as many observers of large institutions have noticed.[6] One incident in particular illustrates how she is able to reorganize the scheduling of routine procedures to suit her needs. One morning I arrived at the Home at 10:30 to discover that Millie was not in the lounge area, the place I usually found her at that time. She had changed rooms the day before and was now located on another floor. I found her in the new room in the process of being dressed by an aide. She said to me: "I've been crying. The system is all changed. Upstairs they got me dressed so early. Here they come much later. I can't stand staying down here so long. It's like a morgue." She clearly needs to be out of her room and in the public, shared space of the lounge and dining areas to feel alive. Within two days of this incident, she managed to get written orders from her doctor stating that she was to be dressed and upstairs by 9:30 so she could participate in the exercise class that took place then. (She had not appeared at exercise sessions before this.) From that time on, she has been dressed by an aide before 9:30.

She also consciously manages the image she presents at various classes and meetings that occur in the Home. The "welcome committee" meets once a week, and Millie walks around for at least an hour before the meeting begins saying to various people: "I want you to come to the meeting today. We have some important matters to discuss." Of the "history class" she states, "The teacher considers me one of the top-notch students." And of the "writing workshop": "The teacher bawled me out for missing a class last week. He says I'm the best in the class, and the class is much more fun when I'm there." She has asserted herself as a leader and an organizer in the Home. She manipulates interactions so that she will be showered with praise by others. She again views herself as competitive. By these methods, she is able to create personal achievements and acquire some of the valued status that has eluded her for so long.

She has recently taken up knitting, an activity that draws several of her themes together. First, it serves as her current form of work (though she is not paid), since it functions in the same way her various jobs did—it fills her time and gives her a specific purpose. Second, it gives her social status. People constantly praise her work, and she has many requests for custom-made objects. She basks in these compliments, which, I observed, have given her eyes new sparkle and her whole being new energy. At last she has found a way to be successful and to be recognized in her community. "I've got enough orders to last me the rest of my life. They're keeping me busy. Everyone wants hats." Third, it is a means to receive more affection and, hence, strengthen affective ties. When Millie makes something for someone, the person invariably throws his or her arms around Millie and says, "I love you." Thus, through knitting, Millie seems to have found a way to fulfill some important lifelong needs.

Millie realized she would have to change her style in order to survive emotionally in the institution. Self-determination is a more optimistic, life-affirming response to her environment than is acquiescence. Through self-determination, she finds ways to cope with her surroundings. Affective ties remain meaningful; Millie understands herself through this theme, and the structure and interpretation of her relationships flow from it. Work and social status, too, remain meaningful as Millie creates a positive self-image and generates as much happiness for herself now as possible.

Ben

Ben has been fighting a battle within himself for most of his 74 years—a battle between his "sober," "steady," "responsible" side and his "carefree," "happy," "romantic" side. One of his major themes is this *dichotomy of self.* He categorizes much of his experience by the struggle between these two aspects of himself and by the way this struggle has influenced his activities and decisions. Ben describes himself in terms of these two character types.

> I *look* in the mirror and I see my father, a very serious guy. My normal, deadpan expression is what my father had, which was a no-nonsense guy who had a big burden on his shoulders. And that's the kind of face I show to the world. But I don't *feel* that way. I feel carefree and happy . . . and I could easily slide or slip into a romantic adventure.

Turning to the sources of this theme, we see that Ben's reference point for the sober aspect of his identity is his father.

He says he resembles his father physically, and this similarity seems to underline for Ben another, more profound likeness—the serious and responsible approach to life. His father was a factory worker who labored long hours most of his life. He had no worker's compensation, and apparently lived in constant fear of potential accidents at the factory or debilitating illness. Ben remembers his father as a nervous man greatly burdened by financial worries. There were six children in the family, and Ben's father felt responsible for giving them all a college education. Through his determination, he did manage to educate his whole family. Ben recalls:

> My father was a molder. It was in the days before there was any compensation. If he had been out of work for a week or month say, we would have been in bad straits. Fortunately, he never was. He raised this big family, but my parents were always oppressed by the dreadful burden of economics. They realized what a frail thing one man's health was—working in a foundry where men were injured every once in a while. And when they were, they were out. They would get $100 or so, and that was it.

Ben says that, until he was a grown man, he did not realize the precarious financial situation his family maintained. He never felt he lacked anything as a child, but his memories of his mother are similar to those of his father: she appears in his life story as constantly worried over how to provide for the family and educate the children.

Like his father, Ben has carried the weight of financial worry throughout his life and has dealt with it by responsible behavior and a grave attitude. Ben's feelings of being heavily burdened apply to other spheres of his life as well. He describes himself during his childhood and youth as "a fearful, nervous person"; he says, "I worried myself sick," and he often thought, "I'll never amount to anything." As a student, he says he was "docile, and well-behaved"; he was not one to rock the boat. Ben took his education quite seriously and imbued it with a profound fear of failure and being "found out to be stupid." Discussions of his youth focus mainly on his education. Looking back now he says that doing well in school gave him his greatest pleasure as a child; failing in a class was his greatest worry. He was strongly motivated to please his parents, and their greatest happiness came from his good report cards. He lived in fear of disappointing them.

At the age of 14, he was sent to a Catholic order boarding school and from that time until he graduated from high school, he was burdened with the decision of whether or not to become a priest. His parents "tried to make a priest" out of him, but he did not want to devote his life to service, and at age 20, he left the order.

Ben continued to express his somber and responsible side as he grew older through the choices he made regarding marriage and career. His wife of 35 years had died several months before I interviewed him. For the second half of his marriage, she was bedridden by a seriously debilitating illness. He describes the marriage before his wife's illness as "mediocre." Their relationship apparently was never fulfilling to Ben. "M. should have married her mother. That was who she was closest to, not me. . . . We were too dumb to go to a marriage counselor." Unsatisfactory though it was, he accepted the relationship: "You don't walk out on something just because it's difficult." When his wife became ill, he felt responsible not only for maintaining the marriage, but also for providing her with all the comforts he could. He hired people to care for her, but he spent much time with her himself, even though he was extremely frustrated by such a limiting existence. He states that he would have been terribly guilt-ridden had he left her when her health began to deteriorate. He chose the loyal, moral response to this situation, and placed devotion to his wife above the gratification of personal desires.

He describes his wife's life after her illness began as "a first-class tragedy," yet he does not see his own life this way. He mentions that other people looking at his life would think of it as "pretty rugged," "sad," or a "rough sacrifice." Possibly, it is the lack of emotional involvement with his wife that has kept her tragedy from becoming his own. Ben perceives the burden of her illness and the care she required as having been a moral responsibility but not as cause for his own suffering.

Of his 30-year job as a bureaucrat in one organization he states: "I was bored out of my skull"; and "I stayed there 20 years too long." One of the reasons he gives for "enduring this boring life" is his duty to support his wife's care. He viewed the job he held as the easiest possible way to earn a living and care for her. He was afraid to quit or to look for something more stimulating and challenging, because he might not be able to meet the financial demands of his wife's health needs.

While telling his life story, Ben stresses his circumspect behavior and his presentation of self to the world as one who had a heavy burden to carry, but one who accepted it with equanimity. His actions and decisions were consistently motivated by his perceived responsibilities, not by his personal wishes. Thus, Ben's "carefree" side has always been submerged; it is rather remarkable that he can *feel* that way now, after a life spent in "doing the right thing."

But he has needed to express his "carefree" side, and his failure to find a way to do so has been his biggest frustration. He feels he paid a great price for the kind of life he chose to live. "I should have . . . I would have longed to have been a stockbroker, or a real estate speculator, or a traveler . . . but I wasn't adventurous enough to quit my job." And later he told me: "I would have given a lot to have been a successful fiction writer. But to write an exciting story you have to experience some things. But my experience—there are no high points, no dramas in it. It's all slow, enduring patience." And his experience is a far cry from the adventurous being who claims to have always wanted a life of risk, romance, and excitement. But Ben was not able to create that life for himself and cannot still, though he has no current moral or financial obligation.

One apparent reason for Ben's inability to express his high-spirited side is his *need for financial security,* a second, strong, motivating theme in his story. As well as contributing to his sober self-image, it serves as an explanatory principle—it accounts for why things have happened the way they have, and it emerges as the basis on which many of his decisions were, and still are, made. The need for financial security has greatly influenced the meaning of success in Ben's life. When I asked Ben what he considers to be his successes and frustrations, he defined two events as his only successes: getting out of teaching and getting to know a particular stockbroker.

Ben talks about his teaching experiences in the context of expanding his horizons, of breaking away from his insulated childhood and youth. He was born in 1904 and raised in a small town in the Midwest, and he attended college there as well. He moved to a larger midwestern city at the age of 24 when he got his first teaching job. He says of that time: "I realized then how timid I was about the future. How shy I was with women. It was only then that I began to date. . . . Arriving in [Central City] was a big thrill for me, a big city life compared to [Small Town]. It was a romance."

Ben taught high school mathematics for 10 years prior to World War II, at which time he was drafted into the army. Ben recalls his army experience as having broadened him further by giving him a new perspective on his profession. While in the army it occurred to him that men who were not as smart as he were earning much more money. He felt he could easily compete with them. "Some of those guys were so dumb they couldn't remember general orders. And they couldn't speak good English. All they knew was how to sell cars or washing machines. I began to realize that at sales, I could make twice as much money as a schoolteacher."

He never became a salesman, but when the war ended, he decided not to return to teaching, which by then bored him. Instead, he moved to the East Coast and was offered a job as a writer in a large corporation. He took the job and held it for 30 years. Not only did he make more money and thus consider himself successful, but he also took a risk—going from what he knew and what was comfortable to the unknown business world. To Ben, who seems quite averse to taking risks, the ability to "venture into one" at all is seen as an accomplishment.

Ben considers meeting the stockbroker a success because it enabled him to double his income through investments. "After I met him, I immediately started making money. And I actually made as much money in the market as I made on the job."

These "successes" are not derived from a sense of inner achievement or self-actualization. Neither are they derived from social status or power gathered in the larger community. Their meaning for Ben is in pure, economic gain. This need has been so strong throughout his life that, though he is financially secure now, when he looks at his past, success is still to be measured in these terms. And though he says that the money he made in the stockmarket gave him "freedom to pursue all my dreams" (i.e., travel, excitement, and adventure), he did not, and still has not, used his economic freedom to realize his fantasies. Not only was his job a disappointment, but he has not used his investment income in a gratifying way. The fact that he can define these experiences as "successful" now, even with hindsight and security, illustrates the power some themes have over time to carry meaning.

To Ben the fact that he never became "a selling writer of

fiction" is one of his great frustrations in life. Although he took writing courses and worked very hard at it, he feels he failed at writing not only because he did not have the personal "experiences" which make a piece of fiction "thrilling," but because he was inhibited by the prospect of competing with other writers.

> If I didn't read what others were writing, I might be dumb enough to think I could sell something. . . . But as I would read something, I'd think, this guy is wonderful. What the hell am I dreaming about competing with him now? . . . I mean, I was third, fourth, fifth echelon down, and the only people who were selling were the top echelons.

Writing for Ben clearly entails competing with people "at the top." He measures success at writing by the amount of money made in selling the product. "That guy probably made $5,000 out of that book. But I never made a dime out of writing." He wrote stories with the idea of selling them. When he realized his stories would not sell, he gave up. And so he has adopted a fatalistic attitude: if he cannot make money writing, he can only be disappointed, for writing serves the need of economic gain. In and of itself it is not gratifying. Ben's need for financial security comes into play here as a basis for evaluating experience, outweighing other considerations.

Religion, a third theme, provides the framework around which he builds his life story. For example, when I asked him to tell me about his childhood, he responded:

> We were brought up in an Irish Catholic family a few blocks away from the parochial school that I attended. My mother was very pious, a very good woman. Worried a lot about bringing up the children the proper way. Both my parents were very proud of my oldest

brother who became a priest, and one of my sisters became a nun. They tried very hard to make a priest out
of me . . . but I was the one who was sort of the black
sheep . . . a good boy, but he didn't take to the
priesthood idea, and what else compares with that?

His orientation in space, his character development, the values he was taught, the description of family members and
family life—all are interpreted through the theme of religion.

The entire account of his early years is structured similarly, with religion at the hub. He sees his life in terms of
closeness to and distance from the religious ideals of his
family. He tells of being sent away to boarding school to
be made a priest, and then of leaving the order. "I lost my
vocation before very long." He did not want to devote his
life to the order, and he was not satisfied with the minimum
amount of education he was to be given there. "I was an intellectual, or thought so at the time, and that's what drove
me out of the order. Had they given me 10 years of schooling
at the time when I wanted it, I would have been a member
yet." His description of himself through these years is based
upon two things: his perception of his relationship to the
order and his interpretation of other peoples' (primarily family members') views of this relationship. Of his leaving the
order he says, "I felt very badly at the time, and I worried a
lot about the effect on my parents." It is evident that the reli-
giously based self-concept of youth has contributed greatly
to the somber side of his identity.

Ben's decision to leave the priesthood was possibly the
most difficult choice of his life. But that decision only temporarily resolved the dilemma of whether or not to dedicate
his life to spiritual goals, for he could not easily dismiss the
deeply ingrained religious values of his parents. In his life
story, religious activities do not emerge as a primary concern
of Ben's middle years. But now, as he speaks of the present

and future, Ben's ambivalence over whether or not to serve some higher purpose manifests itself in a major preoccupation—the need to be generous.

First of all, generosity is a primary value stemming from Ben's religious upbringing. His ideals are the Christian saints, people whose lives were guided by unequivocal altruism. He discusses at great length their charity and compassion in the face of utter poverty. He describes these people as "heroic"; they are most definitely the heroes in Ben's life. For example, Ben said to me: "I read about Mother Therese who has nothing. She goes around and picks up unfortunates in India just so that, for a few hours, or a few days of their lives, somebody cares for them. And she has nothing, earns nothing, only depends on donations in a country where donations must be pretty rare." Ben is not so impressed by anyone he has known personally.

Secondly, Ben has conflicting notions about the part played by generosity in his own self-image. When I asked him what his best character trait is, he stated: "Generosity. Anybody who wants anything that I can give them, including just little things like transportation and time, I do it without question." But as we talked further, it became evident that Ben holds another view as well.

> I don't have this self-giving that other people do. Some
> of my friends will go visit people in hospitals. I admire
> that tremendously. That's what I should do . . . but
> I'm not generous. I've thought to myself often, that's a
> great way to end one's life—doing things for other
> people. That's what I should do, but I'm not going to
> do that, I know it.

He would like to have this heroic quality, but he falls short of his ideal.

Thirdly, the act of giving is strongly influenced by Ben's need for financial security. He says he has "always been too frightened of the economic future to be generous. Lots of causes have come up for which I gave a dollar, when I could have given a hundred." His need to hold onto his resources has conflicted with his religious ideals. At the present time he is financially secure, and his view of how he can be generous reflects this. "I don't do things personally for people, but the money I have I am already dispensing to friends and relatives." This statement also contradicts the giving *self* he describes. Nevertheless, his priorities of giving money rather than time and energy are clearly ordered now, for he says of an acquaintance who talks incessantly, "I haven't got the generosity to listen to him by the hour. I would rather give him $1,000 than listen to him for 1,000 hours."

Generosity emerges now as an important manifestation of the theme of religion in Ben's life. As well as structuring his story, the religion theme provides him with emotional support, more than any person has been able to give him. Religion gives Ben an optimistic outlook on life and enables him to deal positively with the difficult experiences he has had to face. For example, he feels his religious beliefs have enabled him to weather successfully the "tragedy" of his wife's illness and the "perpetual crisis" his life has been in the last few years. He is glad he is religious. "I haven't seen anything else to compare with it. And the friends I have are far less happy than I am with their world outlook and their look to the future. . . . I consider life a big gift. And the next life an even greater one. So, I don't regret. . . . I'm very grateful." Ben's plans for the future center around religious study, for he feels religion will become even more meaningful as he grows older. "My whole quest is to learn more about what does the Supreme Being ask of me for the balance of my life? . . . I will probably start to read more, more conscientiously about religion, because it's the only lasting thing, the only stable thing."

Ben's faith has kept him from being bitter about his empty

marriage and sad, limited domestic situation. Apparently his faith has a positive effect, because his eyes are full of life and he always smiles. He does not look like a man heavily burdened. On the contrary, he *looks* like the "carefree," "happy" person he feels he is inside.

The dimension of timing reveals little in Ben's life story. As Ben talks about his life, no turning points emerge, no periods during which he refocused his priorities or gained a new perspective on himself. To be sure, he has faced transitions at different life stages—entering the army, marriage, a career change, widowerhood—in which he took on new roles and entered into new relationships,[7] but these various behavioral shifts *do not constitute for him* meaningful themes. They have not altered his image of who he is in the world, or his values, and they are not the framework upon which he builds his life story. In fact, these transitions are not discussed as being changes or as representing adjustments. Rather (except for marriage, which he omits), Ben defines his life transitions as he defines the successes discussed earlier: "getting into the army, getting out of teaching, and learning that I could make money in the stockmarket." Transitions that mean something to Ben are those that can be measured in terms of economic gain.

A corollary of the absence of turning points is Ben's style of *disengagement,* a fourth theme. We have already seen that he views his life as "no high points, . . . all slow, enduring patience." No episodes in his life are imbued with affect. Ben's life is monotonous because disengagement runs through it. We see his disengagement in the way Ben describes entering into—and avoiding—relationships.

Ben's life story takes place in an emotional vacuum. He apparently has had no meaningful relationships and, thus, has no reason to register or express emotion. It seems he does not love, hate, feel deeply involved with or committed to anyone. When I asked, "How would you divide your life into chapters?" he said: "I would proceed chronologically—childhood, teenage, employment, retirement. And then have to add chapters on the emotional states." The point here is that, for Ben, emotional states and, indeed, human relations are perceived as something added to life; they do not seem to be an integral part of it.

At no time does he mention the existence of a close personal friend. I asked him who were the important people in his life as he was growing up, and he mentioned a few teachers who stood out as role models for a time. Throughout his adulthood, he has had no strong social ties. When I asked him who he feels closest to now, he replied, "My brother and my sister, that's about it." Neither of them resides in the same city as Ben, but they have come to his aid in recent years, for instance, by helping him reorganize his household after his wife died and by assisting him with other family matters as they have arisen. He summarizes his lifelong attitude toward all relationships: "I tried to avoid complications. I take the easy way out—in personal relationships and other things. Rather than blasting away arguing with somebody about the way it should be, I would rather skip it."

He does not have children. He says: "I had no particular ambition to have children and now I'm glad, because I don't think I would have been a good parent. Much too nervous and worried—like my own parents. I guess that had something to do with it. It would have been a difficult adjustment for me." Looking back, Ben feels he made the right choice: emotional void rather than commitment and complexity in human relations.

Disengagement has led to social isolation. Ben refers to his child self as the "black sheep," the family deviant. Through his youth and early adulthood, he claims he was "timid and fearful" and shied away from involvement with others. He says that even before his wife was ill, as a couple they did not have much of a social life; what little they had nearly vanished when she became bedridden. Now, Ben has "no feeling of closeness" with any of his acquaintances. "There's no intimacy either expected or wanted or anticipated there." And he views his future similarly. "I'll be narrowed down to the time when I will be alone. . . ."

Rather than alter the pattern of isolation, Ben remains passive. I asked him to describe his current daily routine.

> It's a lazyman's day. I go to Mass every day, at eight o'clock, then eat breakfast. Half the time here, and half the time over at the cafeteria down the street, where I usually meet a couple of people that I know. I will come back here and putter around for an hour or so, then down to the "Y" for a swim. Come back and it's time for lunch, yogurt or something like that. In the afternoons, if I don't have a dental appointment or a medical appointment or something, I really can do as I darn please. And mostly it's reading. In the summer I go up to the park and swim again in the afternoons. Gosh. Not much else. My evenings are very poor. I go to the movies a lot, but mostly alone, as I'd rather not fuss around calling someone. I've seen nearly every movie in town. Then I'll hit the sack as early as 8:30 or 9:00. Read until midnight. I don't have a very ambitious life.

In Ben's view, his past was uneventful and boring because he could not create excitement or bring newness into his life. He notes that if "somebody had come along" with an idea, he would "have jumped at the chance," but he could not generate a change in lifestyle by himself. He predicts passivity for his future as well.

> Unless somebody comes along and fires me up with a new enthusiasm, I guess it's going to continue pretty

much the way it is now, a lazy life. Now, it's too bad; I would welcome some enthusiast who would either get me tremendously interested in becoming a great poker player, a great traveler, a great golfer, a great hospital visitor, but I feel none of that. . . . You know, it would be fun to visit a ward full of ex-sailors who have been out to sea, or astronauts, that would be fun. But most people have led lives even more fearful and timid and unexciting than I have.

His disengaged style contributes to both sides of his dichotomy of self—the responsible and the carefree. Lack of emotional investment in people and activities can only make life "steady," "sober," and "uneventful," but it also makes life "carefree." Thus, Ben's interpretation of relationships reinforces and continually recreates his divided self-concept.

Ben's style has contributed to—and is a product of—the pattern of his life course and the way he views himself in different contexts. He has never made a niche for himslf, never "fit" into the situations of which he has been a part. He feels he was an outcast to his family, since he did not want religious training. Teaching did not satisfy him because he could not make enough money. He could not be a writer for lack of "experiences." He was bored and frustrated in his meaningless job as a bureaucrat. His marriage did not fulfill him in any way.

He does not even "live" in his house; that is, he has not made it his own. When he retired, he moved with his wife back to California to the home of his mother-in-law, who had asked him, "Why don't you bring M. here? I can care for her better than you can." I visited him there after his wife and mother-in-law had died. The house was extremely drab and depressing—gray walls, gray furniture. Ben told me that all the furnishings had belonged to his mother-in-law; *his* furniture was in storage. While the two women were still alive, Ben spent most of his time in one upstairs, overcrowded room equipped with a bed, desk, typewriter, television, radio, and books—all the things he needed. At the time of my visits, he still had not "moved into" the rest of the quite sizable house. He clearly prefers to reside in the only space he felt comfortable in during the five preceding years. Now, he is lonely and spends much of his time "puttering around" rather aimlessly, looking for things that might capture his imagination. This is a man whose style plays a great part in the formation as well as expression of identity.

Stella

Whenever I visit Stella in her studio, I am struck by a whirlwind of activity. She is always doing several things at once. This is a busy woman with a full life. I have watched her teach a painting class while at the same time hang a large tapestry on the wall by herself, repair the plumbing under the sink, and pay bills. This much activity at once is typical. Her energy and determination are remarkable. She happens to be 82 years old. She is tall and slim and appears to be delicate. It does not seem possible that so much energy can emanate from such a slim body. One notices her sharp green eyes immediately. When she speaks to someone, her eyes penetrate intensely, but with a gleam of humor. Stella is an artist—the concept of creativity informs the content and structure of her account and all of her themes.

Stella was born in 1897 on a farm in the Deep South, the second of three children. She is able to trace both sides of her family back to pre–Civil War days, when her ancestors emigrated from England. At the time Stella was born, her family was living on "rich" farm land belonging to her mother's kin. Her father wanted to establish his own farm, so they moved to the Southwest and homesteaded. Her fondest, happiest memories are of her early childhood on these large farms. She looks back on that time, though filled with hard work, as the most perfect, blissful existence. The independence and self-sufficiency her father sought and apparently achieved during her childhood is a critical factor in her heritage, and it became a pivotal driving force in her own life.

Her family was extremely close-knit: on an isolated farm, they had only one another to share the chores and provide entertainment, comfort, and support. As a child, Stella wanted to be different from her siblings. She says her sisters were "ladies"; she was a tomboy. They did everything well, wore dresses, played the piano. She would not fashion herself in their mold. Instead, she climbed trees, played with boys, and rode the horses. Her most memorable early relationships were with animals that her father had given to her. She describes her child self as "Li'l Abner."

Stella's formal education began at the age of nine in a "little school house" located about a mile from the family farm. She and her sisters walked or rode their horses to the school every day. Children from several families attended the school, and the teacher boarded with each of the families over the years. Traveling ministers boarded with Stella's family from time to time as well. Stella has vivid memories of going to church every week; her parents were Baptists. She remembers ministers who scared the children with their "hell and brimstone" sermons and members of the congregation who spoke "in tongues." Stella says she memorized much of the Bible at an early age, and she enjoyed reciting Bible stories with her family.

When Stella and her sisters were older, her parents sold the farm and moved to a small town. Stella says there had been a drought for a number of years, and her family couldn't keep the animals alive any longer. In addition, her parents wanted the children to attend high school. During those years, Stella's father owned a variety store and her mother was a cook. When Stella finished high school, she moved several hundred miles away to live with a relative in a larger city so she could establish her own life. There, she attended college, but her education was cut short after about a year when World War I started. She immediately got a clerical job, which she loved because it enabled her to live independently and create her own social life. She was adventurous; she took vacation trips with friends by automobile around the country after the war, traveling through places where no roads existed, camping along the way.

At the age of 24, she moved to Oregon to marry a man she had known for some years. The marriage was brief; her husband left her shortly after her child was born. In the early 1930s, she was poor, divorced, and had a child to raise on her own. She met the challenge. She got a secretarial job which she held for 35 years, was actively involved with her child's art activities, and, deciding to continue her own education, took night courses in science and philosophy. When Stella was 40, her daughter died from injuries sustained in an accident. This tragic event changed the course of her life and turned her into a sculptor and painter.

Now, the one central theme in her life is her *achievement orientation*, especially the need to create art. Stella is future-oriented and goal-oriented, and she is driven by the need to accomplish more and be better. When I told her I was interested in how people reflect back on their lives, she said to me: "I don't look back at all. I only look forward to what I'm going to do next." She does consider her past, however, by competing with it. She compares herself now with the quality of her work and the quantity of her output during other periods in her life. "The only time I look back is when I think, 'I used to do better sculptures and paintings!' . . . Ten years ago I was making more than I am now. I exhibited a lot, and got prizes. I have to get back to work, so I won't have to say that."

Not only does she compete with herself, but she also competes with the other artists and art students who come to the studio she owns and operates.

They were such poor sculptors and potters and painters when they came. And I was so much better. But I didn't do any of my own work because I was busy running the place. And that's when I began to feel bad, because they were learning and catching up with me, and getting ahead of me. Pretty soon, they didn't know I knew anything about art.

Stella needs to be the best at what she does. She needs to have her work highly regarded by others, and she derives fulfillment and self-esteem largely from other people's conceptions of her as a good artist.

But she also needs to meet her own standards of creativity. She says that her greatest pleasure is in "making something" she is pleased with, "accomplishing something." The creative process is inherently frustrating for her, however, as she is never quite satisfied with her work, never quite reaches her goal. When I asked her what she would like to do now more than anything else, she replied: "Make one piece that I'm satisfied with. And I want it to be good, good art. That's all that's important to me now." Her lack of satisfaction with her work is a continual source of frustration.

Stella's achievement orientation and need for recognition apparently have been a part of her identity since her early years, long before she became an artist. When she talks about her childhood and youth, she emphasizes her accomplishments, successes, and failures.

I learned so much at home before I started school that they skipped me from the first to the third grade. . . . I took piano lessons and gave recitals. I did better than anyone else in the county. . . . But one time I forgot everything, so I never gave another recital again.

In great detail she related how she managed to be the third-ranking student in her competitive high school class of 10, how difficult it was for her to go to college, how proud she was of accumulating the appropriate number of credits, how she failed an examination. These are the events of her youth that stand out now.

Achievement provides the framework in which Stella describes her clerical work as well. She emphasized to me how, in her first job, she had to make many copies of everything she wrote and that she "had to be absolutely perfect. I never made an error." Of the secretarial job she held for 35 years she states: "I had a difficult job there—exacting work. And I had to do everything—a lot of responsibility."

In all her endeavors, Stella has wanted to do more, to strive harder, and to be the best. Of the period in her life when she was raising her child, she says: "I wanted to keep myself busy and I always wanted more education, so I went to night school for a few years. It was very stimulating." She has always felt she could tackle more projects and explore more areas of knowledge. Creativity informs a second theme that emerges from Stella's story: her *sense of aesthetics and need for perfection.* This theme serves to define priorities in Stella's life. Her role models for perfection are the two most important people in her life, her mother and her daughter. Everything they did was "beautiful" and "perfect." I asked her to describe her mother. "She was a creative person, an interesting person, a very capable woman, and so pretty! And a perfectionist in everything. Things had to be done just right. And she would never get tired, just going all the time."

Stella describes her mother as a perfectionist where housework was concerned. "I couldn't just drain the dishes, they had to be dried. We had to scald them so they would dry easily. And the clothes had to be boiled in lye. My mother made her own soap. . . . And she was the greatest cook in the world." Her mother was talented in other areas as well. "She was such a good singer . . . and wrote short stories too. . . ." Her mother's seemingly endless ability and productivity have been lifelong guiding forces as qualities worth emulating. Stella states that as she was growing up, she and her mother were like sisters; her mother was only 18 years her senior. Apparently, people told them they looked like sisters, and Stella relished this aspect of their relationship.

Stella's daughter, too, "was good in everything she tried. . . . She was so talented in art. I couldn't imagine where she got it from." Stella describes at length her child's ability to excel in school work. In addition, she was a perfectly behaved child. "I never had to criticize her for anything." Her daughter died at the age of 14—a tragic event which had a profound effect on the development of Stella's identity. The child is frozen in Stella's memory on the brink of maturation and promise. There is only perfection to remember. These memories have become guiding principles for Stella, and since her daughter's death she has tried to act on them. Stella's sense of productivity, beauty, and perfection was first inspired by her mother, later heightened by the way she viewed her child, and finally given supreme value when the child died.

Stella strives for perfection in herself and would like to see others do the same. She said to me: "I think I expect too much of people. I get impatient when things aren't done just right." Her world, like Millie's, may be divided into two sorts of people: those who strive for perfection as she does, and those who are careless and insensitive both to others and to physical objects. She has given me countless examples of the latter type. For instance: "Everyone I know is so clumsy. Why is that? Everyone who comes over here knocks something down. Whenever I serve anyone coffee they knock it over. I never like to use a good tablecloth 'cause I know it's going to get dirty." People "break things" and "mess things up." They impinge on her sense of aesthetics.

All people seek order in their lives. But where they seek order depends upon cultural values and personal priorities. Stella strives for aesthetic order. This is unusual in American society, where most people are concerned primarily with the order of time and objects. Americans put heavy emphasis on precise scheduling, with calendars and clocks to organize time into controllable units. Americans who are not aware of time are considered odd at best, deviant at worst. Indeed, mental health status in the United States is judged in part by whether or not people know what day it is.[8] Stella frequently does not know the date or the time of the day, and she easily forgets appointments. One reason for this is her intense involvement with the task at hand—whether it is teaching a student, writing a letter, or cleaning a closet. Her days are spent in a succession of completely absorbing tasks. The category of time does not usually enter into her activities; it is not relevant to her experience.

One look at Stella's home shows that physical order is not important to her either. Her small apartment is very cluttered. She has trouble finding what she is looking for in the stacks of papers and objects that surround her. Her apartment is filled mostly by art work given to her by friends and other artists. She says: "I know this place is awfully cluttered . . . but I have sentiments. More than most people I think. I don't like to give things up. I always have a special use for each little thing." The meaning of the art objects clearly outweighs the clutter they create. And Stella generally ignores the mess, focusing instead on the beautiful things she creates in the midst of chaos, such as a vase full of flowers or an arrangement of pieces of sculpture she has collected.

Stella's achievement orientation has been channeled into the creation of art works. Her sense of aesthetics and need for perfection are given expression in her creation of aesthetic order in her home and studio. Stella's *need for relationships*, a third theme, is expressed in her creation of roles for herself. With no immediate family now, virtually all the people Stella has known for the past 20 years have entered her life through the doors of her artist's studio. She thus meets most people on an artist-to-artist basis. But Stella needs other relationships as well, and so she has created other roles for herself.

Most of the people who work at her studio are young—in their 20s and 30s. All of the people who work there are at least a generation younger than Stella. These are the people with whom she interacts most of the time; they are simultaneously her friends, children, students, and support network. The problem is that they fulfill all these roles partly, but none of them fully. Stella places a high priority on her relationships with these artists. She says that what she would like "more than anything else would be to have a party and invite all the people who have ever worked at the studio." People come into her life when they arrive to work at the studio for a few months or years, and then disappear from her life when they move away or stop working there. People flow through her life. She grows fond of many of them and would like to keep them close to her. Her collection of sculpture, pottery, paintings, and prints is a symbolic means of achieving this closeness. "I like being surrounded by my artwork. It's like they are my friends. They've all been made by friends." The people may come and go, but their art remains for Stella as a means of keeping friendships alive.

Stella taught some of these people from the time they were small children until they grew up and moved away or went to college. Her eyes light up when she talks about the artistic development "these kids" showed under her tutelage and how they come back to visit her now that they are grown. I observed that her relationships with the young people she has known for years are infused with a warm, nurturing quality. She takes pleasure following their careers and successes as if they were her own children. In a sense they are, because she poured much of her mothering energy into teaching them after her own child died. Teaching children and watching them grow up has enabled her to continue being a mother.

Stella says she has always tried to be a good teacher. She has taught art, in schools and in her own studio, for more than 30 years. She describes the qualities of teachers who most inspired her own work—those who were able to stimulate her creativity "just by throwing out ideas"—and she strives to do that for others. Teaching has always satisfied her tremendously. "It makes you feel like you're doing something worthwhile." She currently feels bereft of this role in light of the progress she thinks everyone at the studio is making and the accompanying feeling she has that people don't need her as a teacher anymore. "I haven't done much art because I've been so busy at the studio. All the people who work here were going ahead of me, and I couldn't tell them anything anymore. So that makes you feel bad, you know." Her achievement orientation is related to her expressed need for the role of teacher/expert. She feels that if she makes more art and invents more techniques, she not only will be a better teacher, but she will also be a better artist, the best in the studio.

As creativity infuses Stella's work, so it also infuses Stella's interactions: she has actively created the roles of friend, mother, and teacher from relationships with people who walk through her studio door. Her support network comes from this group as well. There are no people in her life with whom she feels especially close or on whom she feels she can rely in a crisis. She does not have a support network ready and waiting—relatives or friends she knows she can count on. Instead, her supports emerge at the time of a crisis. Whoever is with her or at the studio when help is needed is the person to whom she turns. For example, her spontaneous support system was called into play when she had an automobile accident several months before I met her. She told me: "After my car was hit, I called the two girls who were working at the studio that night. One drove me to the hospital. The other one drove my car home." If she is ill and cannot run errands, people at the studio offer to do them for her. She is fortunate in that she is surrounded by people who are considerate and who will respond to whatever emergencies arise.

For the most part, however, Stella is extremely self-sufficient. She has maintained the strong independence of her youth. She hates to ask anyone to do anything for her, even in a serious situation. "Sure, these kids will do things for me. They're always asking if I need anything at the store, but I never like to ask anybody to do things. I don't want to inconvenience anyone." She does not want to depend on anyone for anything. The studio is a transient place. Stella alone is its core of stability. Perhaps she does not wish to rely too heavily on others, knowing that they will not be there for her in the future—as friend, student, or support.

Nobody has as much personal commitment to the studio as Stella, and thus, she ends up doing most of the work around the place. Her style of work is *selfless*, a fourth theme in her story. She gives all of her energy to her studio, her art, and the people who come into her life. Stella views her requests of others as "inconvenient"; she refuses to bother anyone. But people are forever bothering her. She has little, if any, time for her own work, and she complains about this. But her sense of responsibility toward running the studio and her priority of giving time and energy influence her behavior. "If somebody wants anything, well, this is my workplace. I feel like I have to. They always look to me to do it. Everybody looks to me to do it." Consequently, her own work is always interrupted or postponed. She gives so much of herself to others that it is hard for her to imagine doing anything for herself. I asked her what an ideal day would be like. She replied: "Well, I would not be interrupted, until I get the most important things done, at least. But that doesn't happen one day in a year, hardly. When I have a day that I can start doing some of my own work, I don't know what to do with myself. I'm just *lost*." Having the chance to do her own work disorients her; she cannot conceive of catering to herself. Self-indulgence does not fit her identity.

Stella's selflessness informs her entire life, not just the running of the art studio. When I asked her to tell me some of the things she does when she is not working, she stated: "I go to the ballet on Sunday afternoons. That's a nice time 'cause it doesn't bother anybody." The art studio is closed then. She would never think of scheduling something for herself if it might conflict with anyone's desire to work at the studio, or if someone might need something from her. All her thoughts and activities revolve around the perceived needs of other people. There are times, of course, when she gets tired of this, when the frustration of not doing her own work mounts up. During those times, she says, "I have either to be selfish, or not selfish." This is a clear-cut issue for her; there is no possibility of compromise in this area.

Stella's selflessness is apparent to me in the way she conceptualizes space: there are no clear boundaries between public and private areas. For one thing, her apartment is located directly behind the studio. She had it built there. A door separates the two but it is usually open. And, the door has no lock. She works both in her studio and her apartment, and moves objects from one space to the other regularly. Artists and students come freely into her apartment to ask questions if she is there. Her apartment is an extension of her studio; it is not conceived as private space. One reason Stella deals with space in this way is to make it easy for people to enter her life. She likes being surrounded by people. She has opened her home and studio so that her relationships can flourish.

Related to Stella's selflessness is her trust in others: her private property is a lending library. She unhesitatingly loans others books and memorabilia that have much personal value, assuming that everyone she meets is trustworthy. When the trust is betrayed, she cannot understand how such behavior is possible. She related several incidents to me in which her assumptions of mutual trust were shattered. For example: "One time, when I was sick for a long time, I had two boys working for me. They just bled me, cleaned me out. Took anything they wanted. Told me they were going to give some of my books to the library. But I bet you they built themselves a nice library. I didn't have enough sense to know what they were doing. I just trusted them." She never directly questioned the boys, nor did she replace the books. She let the matter drop, saying, "I didn't want to be small about it." Even after this incident and others similar to it, she continues to share what she has with relative strangers.

Stella apparently does not change her behavior even when faced with its negative consequences, in this case, loss of property. Perhaps she hopes her selfless acts will foster the relationships she wants to create. On the occasions when she cannot fend for herself and must rely on others for housekeeping and other chores, she does so by opening her life completely. As she has no private domain, everything she owns and everything she is become easily accessible. She says: "You have to be trusting. How can you not be?" As with her selflessness, her trust is absolute. Though she is aware of the drawbacks, Stella does not relinquish her public existence; she perceives it as critical both to the formation of close relationships and to the maintenance of the studio.

The timing of Stella's story is structured around the death of her daughter. This is the critical event in her life, her major turning point, and it divides her story into two distinct sections. The themes described above—her achievement orientation channeled into the creation of art, her sense of aesthetics and need for perfection, her need for relationships, and her selfless style—identify Stella since her daughter died.

Stella's conception of her own development is analogous to the caterpillar/butterfly development process. As the insect has two completely different forms—two identities—which are separated by a metamorphosis, so Stella sees two life stages with a transition period between them. She describes herself during the period before her daughter died as "just a regular housewife. I didn't know anything about anything else. I just sat there while my daughter was studying, and I embroidered and listened to the radio and ironed and washed and cleaned house, doing things you should. I liked it. I didn't know anything about art." She looks back on her pre-artist self as vacuous. She feels she did not have an identity. Then, "My daughter's death changed my life." She describes her own metamorphosis:

> When my daughter died, I needed something to concentrate on, so I started art school at night. I made little things just as she had. But later, after a while, it got to be more and more in me. I was working full-time at the office, but doing my art work every spare moment I had, learning and studying more and more.

She set up her first art studio shortly after her daughter died and began teaching art in the evenings at high schools and colleges and on weekends at her own studio while she was still working full-time. Her energy was ceaseless. When she retired from the secretarial job she held for 35 years, she plunged into expanding her studio, teaching more classes, and doing more projects. Her identity as a sculptor and painter blossomed when she retired from her secretarial job at the age of 62.

She has been expressing her artist self to its fullest capacity for the past 20 years. She has taught several hundred students and launched the artistic careers of many of them. Now, she shows no signs of slowing down or stopping her creative activities. The themes in her life story motivate her to continue by making her life meaningful. They are her understanding of how art and creativity merge to define both who she is and the essence of life.

Three

Structural Sources of Meaning

Events of the past, whether connected with the self or
not, cannot assume conceptual reality unless they are
incorporated in the psychological field of present
awareness. This is only made possible through symbolic
means; past events have to be represented in some
fashion in order to become salient.

A. IRVING HALLOWELL, *Culture and Experience*

The case studies of Millie, Ben, and Stella illustrate ways
in which individuals organize, interpret, and connect
life experiences to become themes and show how themes
may be viewed as building blocks of identity. As they are pre-
sented, these three cases tend to portray the individual as
picking and choosing among idiosyncratic experiences in
order to construct themes and create an identity. But identity
development must also be viewed in its cultural context, as
part of an ongoing and interactive relationship between self
and culture. Themes emerge not only from the individual
perspective but from the play of broader cultural forces on
that perspective—the reality of living in a certain society at

a particular time. Themes are subjective interpretations of one's cultural heritage *as well as* subjective interpretations of personal experience. Themes express the personal salience of growing up, living in, and deriving meaning from a certain kind of cultural experience.

The 60 study participants share two broad parameters of American life, two overriding cultural characteristics: first, their lifetimes span roughly the same historical period, in which World War I, the depression, and World War II are the major national events; second, their background is Caucasian, Judeo-Christian, and ultimately middle-class. In my informants' accounts of their lives, the two wars and the depression do not figure prominently as shaping forces or as direct sources of individual themes. While their common cultural background is an integral part of their identity, its expression in themes is highly individual. In its ideational aspects it provides the common framework for the emergence of dominant values as well as assumptions and expectations about how a life should be lived. In its structural aspects—such as socioeconomic status, family patterns, education, and so on—it provides the setting within which individual choices are made, the limitations and opportunities to which individuals respond in daily life. As my informants told their life stories to me, themes emerged as a way of perceiving those choices in meaningful patterns, and of integrating experience to form an identity.

In this chapter, I will consider why historical events are not essential elements in the life story. Then, I will explore some of the structural forces in the lives of Millie, Ben, Stella, and the other informants to illustrate which ones are perceived as meaningful by these people in their current interpretations of their pasts and how they play a part in the formation of themes.

Perceiving Historical Events

The major historical events in the lives of my informants were World War I, the depression, and World War II. These shared experiences, in and of themselves, do not have a direct impact on identity formulation in late life for this group: historical events are not sources of subjective meaning. For the most part, they are not described as determinants of life course choices or as explanations for personal behavior patterns. To be sure, many of my informants felt the impact of the depression as they struggled financially during this period, and all were affected to some degree by the world wars, depending upon their personal values, political beliefs, and whether or not they served in the armed forces or participated in war-related service activities. Now, as they tell their life stories, they perceive the two wars and the depression as the larger historical backdrop or framework within which they carried on their lives. Most do not perceive these events as personally significant, though they sometimes recall them as part of the setting in which more meaningful events took place.

In 1914, most research participants were between 6 and 19 years of age. Those who were young children simply do not have much recollection of World War I. A few people remember that their fathers or older brothers were away fighting in this war, yet this connection with the event did not have very much personal impact. Some who were 18–20 during the years of World War I terminated their educations and went out to work. They speak of this as an enjoyable time in their lives, filled with the excitement of first independence. Older people, those in their 20s and 30s during the war, had already started in business or the professions or were continuing their educations. Some were drafted, some were not; in either case, the war is not mentioned at all in their accounts of this period of their lives.

In 1929, most study group members were in their 20s and
early 30s. When I asked people to tell me about those years,
very few focused their answers on the depression itself. Although one-quarter of the American work force was unem-
ployed and suffered greatly, none of my informants speak of
extreme personal hardship. Rather, individuals make comments such as, "Everyone was tightening belts all over the
place." Retrospectively, the depression is viewed in general
rather than specific or personal terms.

Only 2 people of the 15 told me that the depression influenced the direction of their lives. One woman was starting
her own business in the early 1930s. She says of that time:

> We started in the depression on borrowed money. Jobs
> we were promised—gone. And I used to wake up about
> four o'clock in the morning terrified. I knew I wouldn't
> starve, but here I was with the rent to pay and no
> visible means of income. So I took to prayer. And that
> quieted me, calmed me, and I began to feel normal.

Because of financial worries, this woman turned to religion
for support, and she has remained deeply religious to this
day. Her business grew during the depression and was quite
successful later. Another woman views the depression as
one link in a chain of reasons why she did not find an interesting occupation for herself. "After college I went into a
very dull clerical job. When I married and came here, it was
the depression, and there was no chance of jobs at that time.
And then when there were more coming, I just didn't seem to
have any drive to do anything about it. . . ."

Many men, some of them husbands of women in the group,
were financially quite comfortable during the depression
years; their businesses or professions did well.[1] One representative comment about those years is from a man who was
in his late 20s when the depression started and had been in
business about five years. "I had a good job and I was am-

bitious. I was going up the ladder. At no time during the depression did I make less than $50 a week. And that was a helluva lot of money then." He and quite a few others from this group were in businesses that grew during the 1930s, or they had jobs that were not severely affected by the dire economic conditions in the country.

During World War II, the majority of these people were in their 30s and 40s. Only a few of the men were drafted or enlisted in the armed forces and fought abroad. For only one of these men who fought in Europe does the war stand out as a critical time in life, a time of extreme crisis that had to be reckoned with personally. "The war was a great crash in my life. I had to become involved because I was in danger. I had to fight fascism for myself and my family. I couldn't ask others to do it for me. It's hard to explain the whole Hitler terror. . . . Our lives were actually in danger. This was a matter of life and death." This man's retrospective response to World War II is unique among this group.

The women generally do not mention the war years as such when discussing their pasts. One exception is a woman whose whole life has been devoted to community service. She was very active with the Red Cross and armed services during the war, and she discusses the activities of this time in her life—her "war work"—in great detail. This woman speaks of "serving the war." She is the only informant who does so.

Many of these people did not have their lives disrupted by the war in any way; they kept their jobs, and their personal lives proceeded as in peacetime. Some relocated or changed jobs during or shortly after the war as new opportunities and situations arose. They mention the war only as a point of reference in time, not as an effective agent in their lives. For instance, one man says, "I had the opportunity to change medical fields right after the war, so I did, as I wasn't happy with what I had been doing." Another man states, "I finally sold the business during the war, and was able to go full-time into public service work."

Millie, Ben, and Stella, too, do not recall World War I or World War II as pivotal forces in their lives. We saw that Stella viewed World War I as an opportunity to earn her independence. When she got her first job, she moved out of her relatives' home into her own apartment. Though the war was on, she describes those years as some of her happiest and most fulfilling. She liked her job; she established her own social life and was very busy. She became engaged twice, explaining: "That's what we all did then to please the boys who were going off to war. It was all propaganda. I broke off the relationships as soon as they returned home." The other women in the study group who were in their 20s during World War I describe those years as Stella does—an opportunity for liberation and autonomy. Stella was a self-sufficient, adventurous young woman anyway. The war gave her the first chance to experience her independence; this was its primary effect on her life. I cannot know the impact of World War II on Stella, because her daughter's death at about the same time (1939) is the critical event which overshadows and colors all memories of those years. She does not mention any war-related experiences, and I cannot infer any from her story.

Although Ben was in his early 30s at the time, World War II had the effect on him that World War I had on Stella—it broadened his horizons, exposed him to different types of people, and changed his ideas about a profession. As Ben interprets it, it was not the fact of war per se that brought about these changes, but the specific experience of being in the army—being thrown into close quarters with people he had never encountered in his sheltered, religious upbringing or college and teaching years—that made him see himself in new ways. For example, his self-esteem was strengthened as he discovered how "dumb" most of the other men were. He began to perceive the narrow focus on his own worldview and background and to fear the future because of these limitations. Perhaps if he had not been exposed to such a variety of men, he would have continued teaching high school and been content with that.

Millie does not even mention the wars in her account of her life. She married her first husband a year or so before World War I began. Looking back now, she views that marriage as the only perfect period in her life, and she does not recall as meaningful or pertinent any war-related details. She mentions only the love in that marriage and the thriving jewelry business. I have inferred from her story that her next marriage took place during World War II and lasted only until a few years after that war. That husband, 20 years her senior, apparently did not serve in the war. Millie's discussion of those years pertains only to the difficulties of that marriage, her children, and her jobs.

Both in relation to other study participants and to other German-Jewish immigrants of her age cohort, Millie's broad life patterns are fairly typical: impoverished childhood in an East Coast urban ghetto, marriage at a young age, relocation to another part of the country to seek better opportunities, prosperity following years of hard work, and a comfortable retirement. However, Millie's life story is unique for this study group, in that she does not relate her experience to the historical events of her lifetime or to a broader social reality at all. The local environment of her childhood—poverty and a large immigrant family—and her moves around the United States provide the only contextual descriptions in her story. Other than the mention of these factors, her interpretive framework is purely personal. Her narrow scope contrasts with the other informants' acknowledgement, however sparse, of the role played by the two world wars and changing social patterns in their personal lives. The lack of contextual material in Millie's account of her past points to the power themes have to establish meaning. Millie's themes have such overriding importance as she relates her life story at age 80 that the larger contexts in which she has lived are of no consequence to her now.

Besides the fact of the two world wars and the depression, Americans over 70 have lived through many trends, fads, and innovations which have profoundly altered the fabric of social life. The lengthy list includes such important arrivals as the automobile, air and space travel, the automation of industry and agriculture, the implementation of social security, radical changes in sexual mores and childrearing patterns, the creation of suburbia, and the concept of the environment as something which can be threatened. As with wars and economic crises, social trends and advances in technology do not figure as main protagonists in the accounts of my informants. They are well aware of the vast changes they have lived through and could certainly talk about them if asked. The point I wish to make is that national developments affecting social life are not viewed as integral to the life story; people are not conscious of these things having a personal impact.

My informants do not set their stories on the stage of history, neither do they view themselves as makers of history.[2] Perhaps only those whose lives have been drastically interrupted or permanently altered by larger historical processes which they can identify (for example, survivors of the Holocaust or prisoners of war) can perceive themselves as actors in and products of historical events.

Erikson (1975:113–168) draws attention to the relationship between an individual's life story and larger historical processes by describing four conditions under which an autobiography emerges. His analytic scheme is useful for understanding why historical events do not have greater significance to my informants.

One condition of the autobiography, according to Erikson,

is the relationship between the *individual* and *specific moments* or events in his or her life. Examples of this type of relationship from my informants' accounts would include Millie's move to the nursing home, Ben's decision to leave the priesthood, and the death of Stella's daughter. Each of these discrete moments had an impact on the direction of the informant's life course and subsequently on the shape of the life story. Specific moments account for uniqueness in every story.

A second condition of the autobiography is the relationship between the *individual* and *sequences of events* in his or her life. For example, we recall that Millie worked at various retail and clerical jobs for most of her life, both to make a living and to free her mind from dwelling on the problems she faced. For Ben, career choices at various junctures were determined by his overriding financial insecurity. Stella has created, expanded, and continued to maintain a viable studio environment in which she can develop as an artist. As particular moments or events in a person's life are unique, so too are the sequences of events in a life. As they are retold, they are expressed as meaningful, logical, and integral to one's sense of self when one looks back over one's life course. Millie's overall work experience, Ben's lifelong career limitations, and the maintenance of Stella's art studio are not merely sequences of events that these individuals impartially recall. We have seen that each sequence is meaningfully constructed as the life story is told in order to give shape and substance to the account and to give identity to the autobiographer. The "true" sequence of moments in a life—how events actually happened—is inaccessible to the researcher, because he or she was not there as the moments unfolded, and because events are reconstructed and reinterpreted at the time the life story is told in order to have relevance and salience at that instant for both the teller and the listener.

A third condition under which the autobiography emerges is the relationship between a *moment* in the individual's life and the larger *community* or cultural setting in which that moment occurred. One of the few examples of this type of relationship from Millie's story is her description of walking to her piano lessons through the poor, immigrant neighborhood of her childhood. This single act is recalled so vividly because it allowed Millie to symbolically escape from her local cultural context and merge with the idealized American middle-class community. Ben gives us several illustrations of this type of relationship in his account—for example, his decision to become a teacher rather than a priest in order to sever his ties with the all-pervasive and claustrophobic religious community of his childhood. Stella, too, gives us a few examples of the relationship between *moment* and *community* in her life—for instance, the timing and circumstances of World War I which enabled her to get a job and lead an independent life.

Erikson's fourth condition of the autobiography is the relationship between *sequences of events* in the individual's life and *larger historical processes*. Millie, Ben, Stella, and the other research participants offer no discussion of this aspect of their lives.

The 15 life stories I collected focus upon Erikson's first two conditions—the relationship between the individual and specific moments that shape the life course, and the relationship between the individual and sequences of events. My informants defined these relationships as they constructed their stories.

As we have seen in the stories of Millie, Ben, and Stella, informants did offer occasional descriptions of the relationship between specific moments in their own lives and the larger community or cultural setting in which they occurred—Erikson's third condition. But discussions of this type were rarely detailed or lengthy, and they never dominated an account. Moreover, no research participant talked about the patterns of his or her entire life course in terms of their connection with larger collective developments—Erikson's fourth condition. In his analysis of Gandhi's life (1969, 1975: 111–190), Erikson points out that Gandhi consciously interacted with—and in fact deliberately grappled with—the historical and cultural circumstances of his local environment and entire nation, both as he lived his life and as he created his autobiography. One reason Gandhi's life story fascinates scholars from so many disciplines is that it offers researchers detailed descriptions of the relationship between the sequence of events in one life and the broader cultural setting in which they occurred. Perhaps only great men and women—those who are motivated to write autobiographies by the sense of their own impact on history—can consciously construct their accounts to explain relationships between personal development and historical processes. For the rest of us, our sense of choice—of the self interacting with its cultural context—stops far short of major historical events.

Sources of Meaning from the Past

If national historical events are too remote to serve as sources of subjective meaning, how meaningful are social structural factors—the conditions to which individuals respond in daily life? As my informants tell their life stories, details of certain social structural factors emerge again and again in their accounts; often two or more factors interact closely. Other factors are mentioned only occasionally, or not at all. The socioeconomic status of childhood (whether impoverished or middle-class), family ties, education, geographic mobility, and work figure prominently and most often in the life stories I collected. These factors now appear as meaningful contexts for the creation of the life story. On the other hand, motherhood (or fatherhood) and childrearing experiences are not emphasized by the informants; in some cases they are hardly mentioned. They do not loom large as sources of themes or essential components of identity. Religion, though incorporated into themes by a few people, is not directly a source of meaning for most.

Certain structural factors appear to hold meaning for many members of the group as a whole, reflecting their common cultural background. But exactly what meaning a given factor yields varies widely from one individual to another, depending on how it interacts with other factors in a person's life. Structural factors in the life story do not in themselves illuminate fully the dynamic relationship between identity and cultural context, but they do illuminate one key aspect: the limitations and opportunities a person has faced, the choices made accordingly, and the meaning drawn from those choices as it emerges in themes.

We turn now to some social structural factors that emerge from the texts as sources of meaning and to ways in which they affect the creation of the life story. Again, the actual structural factors that impinged on the lives of informants cannot be known by researchers analyzing retrospective accounts. Instead, informants identify factors which are currently meaningful.

All informants talk about the influence of money, or lack of it, on their youths. Though all members of the study group are middle-class now, their economic backgrounds vary greatly and have fluctuated over their lifetimes. About one-quarter came from affluent homes. Their fathers were in the professions or were successful businessmen; some of their mothers inherited wealth; some had servants in the family household. This is how one woman explains her position in her childhood household: "In my generation, the children were relegated to nurses. I was subjected to a nurse for seven years. . . . I was a spoiled child—a brat. I never had to do anything, and I never learned to do anything because the maids did it all." This kind of explanation typifies several accounts of childhood experience.

Another quarter of my informants were quite poor during their youths. Their fathers had unsuccessful business ventures or struggled with farming. These people had specific duties and jobs to perform in the household from a very early age and felt a strong responsibility to contribute to the family welfare. One man who grew up on a farm says: "My father died when I was 15. From then on I was the main support of my mother. I was going to school and I worked on the farm too. In those days, I worked very hard." A woman from a large, poor family relates: "I had to help my mother do everything from when I was very young. I remember beating the rugs . . . and she held me out the windows while I washed them. . . . When I was a little older I would take care of all the children in the neighborhood to earn money."

Most study participants grew up in middle-class households. They had no financial responsibilities to their families, and their accounts of childhood and young adulthood reflect this; they focus mainly on social experiences, friendships, recreational activities, part-time jobs, and relationships with family members. One typical reflection back to youth comes from a woman with a middle-class background. "The high school years were some of the happiest years of my life. We had a nice group of friends, we did everything together, shared everything . . . and life proceeded. We graduated from high school and went to college. We were supposed to earn a living and we did. . . ." A man whose parents were professionals sums up his childhood thus: "During my childhood I was a big profiteer. I had a paper route, bought them for 10¢ and sold them for 15¢. . . . Then I joined the Boy Scouts and had a lot of fun with that." Another woman states: "I had a gang in grade school. . . . I was ambitious. I got good grades and worked hard and so forth. One time I wrote a speech and won a prize. . . . And there were lots of parties then. . . ." These descriptions are typical for at least half the members of the study group.

Millie did not dwell on her impoverished childhood in our conversations; yet she alluded to it often enough to reveal that it is significant in the formation of some themes in her life. For instance, we have seen that she has always craved social status. Her vibrant description of the social meaning of piano lessons when she was young illustrates how she struggled for status throughout her life but was rarely able to achieve it. The need for higher social status remains salient in her old age, and since she realizes she cannot acquire it through her own devices and did not acquire it through birth, she tries to claim it now through association with affluent people.

Poverty is interwoven with ethnic background in Millie's account of her past. Millie's parents were immigrants, a fact with which she has never felt comfortable. In one breath Millie told me that her mother was German, but that she was "thoroughly Americanized, she didn't speak with an accent or anything." She wanted to make sure I understood that, although her parents were from another country, they were as much a part of the melting pot as possible. Millie appears to have been ashamed of her parentage as she was growing up, and she yearned to be part of some idealized, purely American culture. The immigrant status of the family was, of course, tied to their poverty and has fueled Millie's lifelong strivings for status and affluence. The piano lessons, in addition to symbolizing higher economic status, also symbolize her break from the traditions of her "peasant" parents. Through the lessons, she was initiating an activity truly her own.

Poverty in childhood is cited by other members of this study group (not only immigrant Jews) as the critical factor motivating them to become financially successful. Many informants told me that, in their youths, they promised themselves they would not have to struggle to put food on the table all their lives as their parents had struggled. Stories of people with meager beginnings rising to prominence in their professions or businesses are common in this group; for many, their progress toward higher economic status is an important source of meaning.

It is possible that Millie would be affluent now had her first husband lived longer. Although after he died she married twice to gain economic security and the status she felt would accompany it, she was not able to sustain her periods of prosperity into old age. Thus, the poverty of her youth and her lifelong financial insecurity have contributed to her need, currently expressed in themes, for status, acceptance, love, and attention.

Ben's insecurity, expressed in financial rather than emotional terms, also got its start during his childhood through the emotional climate that pervaded his household, if not through actual poverty. Though his father was present and provided the basic necessities for the family, both his parents were apparently always anxious that some catastrophe might topple their precarious economic footing. Ben grew up in an environment of tension and nervousness. He observed and learned only two responses to the hardships of life—worry and religious faith. We have seen how these two behavior patterns, established early, have influenced his decisions throughout life and into old age. They have been the source of his frustrations and shaped the themes through which he now expresses himself.

In contrast, Stella was quite poor during her young and middle adulthood, which took place during the depression, but she vividly remembers her secure early childhood and talks about it at length as the happiest time in her life. She describes her family as close-knit, loving, and always available to her in those early years. She grew up in a relatively small family, quite isolated from other households in the rural Southwest. Family members spent much time together, working the farm and providing support and entertainment for one another. During her childhood the family was a stable unit, full of love. The security established in this environment probably contributed to her ability to cope well with the hardships she later faced, first as a divorced woman with a child to support, and then when the child died. In addition, it probably enabled her to recover from that tragedy and go on to express herself in the creative sphere.[3] Thus, economic status has had relatively little importance to Stella because of the presence of another factor that is more meaningful in her life story—close family ties.

Another structural factor that accounts for the difference between the early family life of Stella and that of Millie and Ben is the rural/urban contrast. In isolated farming households when Stella was a child, relationships had to be amiable for the family to survive; there was nobody else for miles around to provide a support network. In addition, farm family members shared the specific tasks and overall goals of making the farm a viable concern. Urban family members generally do not now, and never did, share as many activities as rural family members. Urbanites' survival as a family unit does not depend on complete interdependence, and subsequently, their lives are not as intertwined. In an urban setting, the peer group and work environment potentially provide greater support, companionship, and distraction than the family.

In Stella's story, the close-knit family emerges as a positive factor which established her security. Millie needed that closeness but apparently did not have it, because her family concentrated their attention on the outside world and had little to give her: her father was out late gambling, her brothers were away working, her sister was at her singing lessons. In Ben's story, the family is described as united by religious goals which he did not share. His feeling, established as a child, of being an outsider has remained with him and contributed to his theme of disengagement. And his inability to express religious faith in the manner his mother wanted of him and as his siblings did set the stage for frustration in various spheres of endeavor.

Memories of and attitudes toward parents reflect a common quality of family life among the study group. Descriptions of parents emerge regularly and are remarkably consistent. Mothers are described as "pious," "charitable," "remarkable," "active," "gorgeous," "brilliant," "very good," "devoted," and "perfect." Without exception, mothers are remembered in superlative terms, and they embody all the positive values of mainstream American culture during the time my informants grew up. Fathers, on the other hand, are not described in as much detail or in such a positive way. They were "ordinary," or "not there very much." Memories of them generally are not as vivid and not invested with emotions as are memories of mothers. Some typical remarks about fathers are: "He didn't communicate"; "He didn't tolerate children"; and "He was cool towards me." In retrospective accounts, these people idealize their mothers and recall having close relationships with them. By and large, fathers are remembered as emotionally distant: "I didn't know him too well"; "not worth emulating"; "He was uneducated"; and "He strayed from the beaten path." In the informants' accounts, mothers provided both the moral and physical backbone of family life. Fathers came and went, and are not thought of by these people in terms of a positive contribution to family life.

Despite the idealized role they assign to their mothers, their own role as mother is never prominent in the retrospective accounts of my female informants. Maintenance of close family relationships emerges as a dominant value for all informants, but specific events concerning childrearing and the process itself are not of prime significance to these women now when they discuss who they are and how they have spent time. They see themselves as having a variety of roles and being multifaceted people, even during the child-rearing years. Relationships with husbands and friends, the development of character traits, and successes and frustrations in the larger social world play a greater part in their life stories than do childrearing and family life.

Education occupies a relatively important place in the stories of all informants. One reason for its prominence in these autobiographies is its historical role in American society. The sociologist Robin Williams (1970: 282–322) notes the widespread "faith in education" which has characterized America for over a century and which is upheld primarily by two notions: first, that a democracy requires an educated citizenry to participate in public decision-making, and second, that education brings economic reward plus social status to the individual and security to the nation.

Autobiographical material I collected attests to this faith in education. Descriptions of childhood dwell at length on the need to do well in school, fears of disappointing parents with bad grades, frustration over academic failures, and the sense of pride in academic success. Educational achievement was a primary value in most people's families while they were growing up. The retrospective accounts of my informants stress the belief that education would lead to occupational success, economic reward, and/or higher social status. Besides being a means to an end, education also is viewed by most informants as being intrinsically worthwhile. Two-thirds of this group attended college, and some attended professional school as well.

From the stories of Millie, Ben, and Stella, I learned that education was valued in their families, both for its intrinsic merits and for the rewards it could bring. But in each case, historical factors and family situations played a part in the amount and type of education each person received as a child and young adult, the attitudes which accompanied schooling, and the memorable aspects of the education process. When I asked Millie to tell me about her childhood, the first thing that came to her mind was going to school. Again, here was an opportunity to get away from her "foreign" parents and join the melting pot. Education as a factor in her life story interacts with ethnic background, as does economic status. Education also created opportunities for affiliation: school meant peer group, and Millie emphasizes that her girlfriends from the elementary years were her closest confidants through the period of her first marriage. It is interesting to note that though she wanted to separate herself from her European heritage, and her childhood neighborhood was ethnically heterogeneous, her four closest school friends were also from German-Jewish immigrant families.

In high school, Millie took business courses because her family needed her to work. At 16, she had to quit school and get a job to contribute to the household. Her eldest brother placed her in her first job as bookkeeper and stenographer in a jewelry store. The historian Tamara Hareven (1978a,b) notes that during the early years of this century, when Millie was young, the family played a much greater role than it does today in the determination of individual pursuits. During the nineteenth and early part of the twentieth century, most families functioned as economic units. Thus, the timing of transitional events (such as marriage) and choices of education or employment were structured around the family's need to survive and opportunity to prosper. This social fact certainly shaped the type and length of Millie's education and, indeed, much of her future. The kind of schooling she received and the timing of her transition from student to employee were determined by the economic status of her family, not by her own desires. Millie says she enjoyed all the subjects she studied in school. I do not know her feelings about the termination of her schooling, because, as she recalls that life period now, meeting her first husband in the jewelry store stands out as the critical event. Ending her formal education has no special meaning.

In contrast, education emerges as a pivotal factor in shaping Ben's entire life story; it is one explanation for the course his life has taken and the development of his identity. Though he emphasizes religion as the key theme in his life story, he talks about his childhood and early relationship to his parents in terms of education as well. For example, his self-image, his fears of failure and notions of success, his worries about pleasing his parents—all are defined through his schooling. I asked Ben to describe himself as a child. He replied, "I was a good student." When I asked him what gave him the most pleasure and what upset him most during his early years, he answered: "Schoolwork. My parents reinforced that. If my report card was good, they were happy. And when I flunked arithmetic, they weren't happy. . . . School was very important. That's about all I could have failed at."

Ben describes the type of education he was given as limiting his social development and as contributing greatly to the somber side of his identity. He was sent to a small Catholic boarding school at the age of 14. There, for four years, he was heavily burdened and totally preoccupied with the decision of whether or not to become a priest, to accept the choice made for him by his family and superiors at school or to break away. His education and life at school were purely serious business; he recalls no fun, pranks, friendships, or excitement. The cloistered, religious, all-male environment did not give him any social skills with which to negotiate the secular, male/female world outside. He graduated from high school frightened, extremely shy, without friends, and without a support structure when he decided not to become a priest. His education experience contributed to his sense of social isolation and his inability to establish meaningful relationships.

On the other hand, Ben's higher education was the vehicle through which he escaped the priesthood. He thought of himself as an intellectual, not as God's servant; this self-concept motivated him finally to reject the path on which his parents had placed him and go on to college and the teaching profession. He says of that life period: "I had a great yen for the intellectual life. If somebody had offered me a job, if I could have gotten a Ph.D. and been a professor for the rest of my life, maybe I would have been happy, I don't know."

We recall that Ben conceives of his life without turning points. This is the only place in his account where he speaks of a potential turning point, an opportunity that he missed. But in the same thought, he goes on to justify his lack of a Ph.D. and nonacademic career through his theme, the need for financial security. "I doubt I would have been happy. In the academic life, they're terribly concerned about money, until they get to be tenured professors. It's not a nice relationship. . . ." The irony, of course, is that, though he chose a job that offered financial security, he has continued to worry about money his entire life and to regret the "boring" lifestyle he chose. His continued ambivalence over an academic career highlights the need for him to explain why he did not take a chance and pursue something which might have satisfied him. Education allowed him to escape the priesthood, but it did not, ultimately, aid Ben in finding a satisfying niche in the world.

For Stella, education has been a vehicle through which she expresses her competitive spirit, her drive to accomplish, and her desire to become a better artist. She attended small country schools; there were only ten students in her graduating high school class. Yet, her educational horizons were always broad, and her parents encouraged her ambition. As a youngster, she competed in music contests and gave recitals all over the county to school and church groups. When she graduated from her academically limited high school, she decided to move to a larger city for another year of school so that she could take necessary courses for college. Proud and excited to have been accepted to college, she began the year World War I started. She observed her sister and some of her friends getting war-related jobs and earning more money than they ever had before. She decided that she could do the same and that the war was an opportunity for her to create an independent life. So she quit school, took some business courses, and immediately got a relatively high-paying clerical job.

College attendance was atypical for women of Stella's age cohort. Yet, it was not unusual for the female participants in this research. World War I encouraged the emancipation of women from solely domestic roles because they were needed by industry to serve the war effort. The war itself coincided with the young adulthood of about 20 members of the study group; its subsequent repercussions on social life were felt by all study participants. To be sure, the newly acclaimed freedom from traditional female roles was felt, to a greater or lesser degree, by all American women of Stella's cohort. But for study participants, this cultural phenomenon was coupled with the strongly instilled value of formal education. Most of the middle-class women I interviewed spoke of their youthful independence in terms of the desire to attend college. Some were able to do so, at least for a year or two. Others were not allowed to go to college because of family resistance. Others, though wanting to continue their educations, married instead.

Stella's desire to continue her education reemerged about 10 years after the war ended when she was both working and caring for her child. She read voluminously on her own and attended night school for several years, where she wrote papers and engaged in lively seminars and debates. Over the years, she acquired a solid, well-rounded liberal arts education. A complete set of the *Great Books of the Western World* (Hutchins 1952) is in her library; she has studied most of them. More than other informants, she has pursued her formal education over the years.

After her child died, Stella channeled her desire for learning into the study of art. Her art teachers have been the most influential people in her life (aside from her mother and daughter), since they knew how to nurture her artistic self. To them she owes the development of her aesthetic sense as well as her technical training.

Thus, education is a rich source of meaning for many members of this group, and one that operates in a variety of ways. Part of its force is ideational: educational achievement was a primary value in most of my informants' families, and a standard for measuring success or failure. As a structural factor, it interacts in the life stories with other factors and with themes. In Millie's case it provides part of the setting in which more meaningful aspects of her life are expressed: her need for affiliation, her ethnic background, her family's economic status. For Ben it is closely intertwined with key aspects of his identity: as a locus for success, as a socially isolating experience, as an alternative to religion, as a setting in which his need for financial security is expressed. For Stella it is a vehicle for liberation and growth, an opportunity for her to express and develop key aspects of her identity.

Geographic mobility is frequently mentioned in people's accounts, and it figures largely in Millie's story. However, Millie moved more than most informants—more than 10 times in her life. She moved each time she married and when each marriage ended; she moved for her own health and that of a child and a husband; she moved to be close to her children; and finally, she moved when she could no longer care for all her needs. An interpretive pattern emerges as she talks about these moves—they were *all* dislocations, forced upon her by others or by external circumstances, not moves she made out of personal choice. It is easy to see how this mobility, viewed negatively as being brought about by outside forces, contributes to her acquiescence theme.

Even her first move away from home, to live with the man she loved, is seen now as traumatic and not of her own choosing. "We went to live in another city because he had this job there. I had never been away from home; I was a little homebody. I got very upset living there. It was like living in Europe, away from home. I became ill and was brought back to my mother. . . ." She moved during her second marriage because that husband wanted to be away from her children; the move did not improve their relationship. During her third marriage, she moved several times, in search of a better climate for her sick husband, but the moves did not improve his health and only exhausted her and disrupted her employment.

Millie relocated several times after her third husband died; she was "pulled" from place to place, and her children "decided" where she should go. Each move represents a major upheaval in her life, and she has had many. The moves, instead of resolving tension and providing comfort, have only contributed to her sense of not being in control of her own fate.

In contrast, most other informants express geographic mobility as a positive force in their pasts. For both Ben and Stella, mobility provided an opportunity for them to seek their fortunes and make something of themselves in the world. Mobility was a key to freedom and independence. However, Ben was unable to fully experience the freedom mobility offered him. True, his move away from home to attend college gave him independence from the oppressive religious influence of his family. But his subsequent moves, which accompanied the transitions in his life—teaching, army, marriage, job—did not give him freedom in any sense. He could not take the opportunity mobility offered him in those earlier years, because the "sober," "steady," "burdened" side of himself was too powerful. And it is still too strong to allow mobility to have much impact on his behavior: though he now wants to travel and realize his "carefree" side, he is unable to do so. He currently talks about visiting South America and Europe, but he has not made any specific travel arrangements: his passivity overrules his free spirit.

Stella moved away from home at the age of 18 to attend college and support herself. At the age of 24, she journeyed across the western states to Oregon. As a young woman, mobility allowed her to be adventurous and express her independent self. She describes her trip west as though she were an early American pioneer—"just like the covered wagon days." She traveled by car with some cousins; luggage was jammed everywhere. The trip took six weeks. For much of the distance, there were no roads, and Stella recalls traveling through the desert of the Southwest, seeing cow skulls and bones along the way, and driving right through flooded streams. She and her companions passed few towns and carried their gasoline in cans. Stella fondly remembers this adventure; she particularly enjoyed meeting people wherever they stopped to camp and wearing trousers and smoking cigarettes during the journey—the ultimate signs of liberation during that era.

Stella married in Oregon and did not return to the Southwest except for brief visits to see her family. After her child died, geographic mobility ceased to be relevant, because she developed a meaningful way to express her autonomy fully through her artistic pursuits and nonconformist lifestyle.

Religion as a structural factor—its practice, denominational affiliation, participation in organized activities, and the like—is not a commonly held source of meaning for these people, though it does emerge as a theme for several study participants. Ben's emphasis on the role of religion in his life is extreme.

The shared, Judeo-Christian background of this group has

a variety of religious expressions. No one specific religion dominates; Catholicism, Judaism, and a variety of Protestant denominations are represented. About one-third of these people were raised in very religious households. For them, religion permeated all facets of youth and was one of the strongest factors in childhood socialization. It served as the guide to proper behavior. One man says: "I was raised a strict Calvinist. My mother embraced that rather uninviting religion and pushed it off onto me. I was scared to death by it. . . . I was pretty square. This Calvinism included the idea that dancing and other things were of course very sinful. So I didn't do them." A woman says: "I was raised Catholic. And I took it very seriously. We had to go to church before we went to school in the mornings. Nobody would wake me up, and I became a nervous wreck training to wake myself up so I had time to go to church. That's why I became pretty anxious and nervous." These two people and most of the others with strict religious upbringings rejected their religions shortly after they left home. They now consider themselves agnostics or atheists. Only a few people who were raised in very religious households consider themselves quite religious at present. Another third were raised in what may be called moderately religious households. This group includes Jews, Christian Scientists, Baptists, and other Protestants. These people studied the Bible as children, attended Sunday school for varying lengths of time, and went to church regularly or occasionally with their families. The remainder of the study participants were raised in nonreligious households.

Most of these people do not consider themselves religious now, though there are a few who participate regularly in the rituals of their faith. For the most part, these people identify themselves as Jews or Christians, but they attend church or synagogue infrequently, if at all, and the organized practices or philosophies of their faiths hold no special meaning as they tell their life stories now. Religion as a structural factor generally is not a direct source of meaning (Ben's case is exceptional), though the Judeo-Christian heritage shared by this group is an important part of their cultural context.

My informants' descriptions of the meaning of occupation in their lives fall into two broad categories. For about half of the study group, work was something that had to be done and it never provided much satisfaction. Other aspects of life such as family relations or friendships hold much more meaning. For others, especially those with professions, the work role has been a primary source of identity, and occupational achievements have been the main source of gratification and positive self-esteem.

With only three exceptions, all research participants entered the labor market when their formal educations ended. Many earned money on a part-time basis while they were still in school. About two-thirds of the men were in business; the others were in the professions. Most of the women did office work—accounting, bookkeeping, secretarial, clerical—for at least a part of their occupational lives. A few were teachers. Some of the women were very active in their communities, especially during the years of World War II, and they worked as volunteers for church groups, schools, the Red Cross, and other community organizations. Half of these people built a profession or a business over a lifetime; most of them have resided in this urban metropolitan area since they began working as young adults. The others changed jobs at least twice over the years, either when they relocated or when the needs of their families changed.

Those who were heavily invested in their occupations define the successes and failures in their lives in terms of their jobs and describe themselves in terms of occupational roles and work habits. Often the influential people in their lives have been professional mentors or peers. I asked a 78-year-old semiretired lawyer to describe what he was like at the height of his career. He replied: "I was very busy. I did a lot of night work, weekend work. Was very dedicated to my practice, which I enjoyed. . . . I had a lot of fire and ambition. That's about all I could say for myself." This man still goes to the office daily, though his work load does not require it, because the continuation of his professional affiliation means more to him than participation in any other activity.

His total and ongoing identification with his profession is in marked contrast to that of another man who was in public relations for 30 years. At age 72 this man says:

> I could have hung onto my job a little longer if I had wanted, but I was 65, and decided to knock it off. It would have been economically advantageous if I had hung on a little bit longer I guess. But I wanted to do other things. See, I always considered myself an actor, and since I retired I can devote time to it.

This man has never seen himself in terms of his work role, and his career did not dominate his life. His occupation is not mentioned when he discusses the important people or events in his life. He currently derives great pleasure from and spends much time participating in a neighborhood theater group. These contrasting opinions represent the extremes in attitudes toward work held by my informants.

Thus about half my informants took their jobs seriously and were conscientious workers, but they now view work in a limited context and put occupational roles in the broader perspective of a lifetime of other kinds of experience. For them, work is not a rich source for forming identity in old age. For the others, past jobs or work roles are an important source of subjective meaning. For Millie, work—defined as consistent employment—is the vehicle through which she acquired and has maintained self-esteem and success in the larger world. For Stella, work is the expression of her creative self.

Sources of Meaning from the Present

What current conditions are important sources of meaning for this group? When my informants talk about the present, three factors provide the context for their discussions: activity and productivity in the daily routine, family ties, and friendship. We have seen how these factors contribute directly to the formation of themes in the lives of Millie, Ben, and Stella. The importance of family and friends emerges in Millie's key theme, affective ties; it is expressed in Stella's theme, the need for relationships, when she talks about the roles she has created. In contrast, Ben's lack of emotional commitment to people emerges in his theme of disengagement and the "carefree," unattached side of his divided self. Activity and productivity find direct expression in Stella's achievement-orientation theme. Millie's current activities of knitting and attending classes and meetings in the Home find symbolic expression in her themes of work, social status, and self-determination. Ben's passivity—his inability to invest in any activity—is part of his disengaged style and dichotomy of self. His lack of worldly activity reinforces the importance of religion as the only meaningful endeavor in his life.

Current health is a fourth factor that is not a source of meaning in itself but that greatly influences the extent to which activity and productivity can be realized in the individual life. Two-thirds of the study population considered themselves to be in good health during the fieldwork period. Many of these people have some health problems that prevent them from leading as full a life as they would like—for instance, several are quite hard of hearing, one is blind, some tire very easily and cannot walk much or walk laboriously with canes, some have trouble with arthritis or muscular pain, others have heart disease—but nevertheless, they have adapted to their specific physical situations and continue to lead active, rich lives in spite of certain limitations. When discussing their routines and activities with me, they never mentioned their health. It was discussed only if I asked about it. As with younger people, the good health of these people is taken for granted and does not arise spontaneously as a topic of conversation.

The remaining third, including those who are institutionalized,[4] lead moderately restricted lives. Although none is bedridden, chronic health problems or a general feeling of weakness or fatigue prevents them from being as active as they once were and would still like to be. Their physical health limits their daily routine and choice of activities, and this causes varying degrees of frustration. Several people are restricted in their pursuits by the poor health of a spouse.

A 92-year-old woman who considers herself to be in fairly good health is restricted by both her bedridden husband and her own lack of energy. She describes her routine in relation to these limitations:

> I'm ambulatory and I drive a car. In the morning I do
> the household marketing and the family cooking.
> These two occupations are the most I can undertake as
> I tire so easily. But in relation to some of my contemporaries, I realize how fortunate I am to be able to function as I do. I conduct two classes still and have people
> in to visit. . . . But the late afternoon drags on slowly
> until it's time to prepare dinner. I'm glad for this as it's
> time-consuming. I'm housebound in part because of
> my husband. I'm fortunate that I can have the nurses,
> but I'm still "on call" some of the time. My daughter
> says, "Why don't you go out more?" But I can't walk
> any appreciable distance. Recently, when I went to the
> park, I was so exhausted that I decided such outings
> were no longer in the cards.

An 82-year-old woman who lives alone calls herself a semi-invalid. She described her activity level to me:

With my heart and other problems, I have to take care. I don't drive anymore and I don't dare take walks since I fell. I have a driver twice a week. I go to very few social events. At a party the other night, I got dizzy and had to go home after half an hour. . . . Most of my life now is involved in just keeping going. I'm taking medication for this and for that; I have to rest a lot. I don't travel anymore—I'm not interested. I won't go very many places. I'm more comfortable in my own apartment—I saw my doctor a couple of weeks ago. I told him I was getting awfully tired of all this jazz. I know the future is not going to be too long.

The restricted lives led by these two women are typical of about 20 members of this group.

Restricted or not, informants spend their time *doing* things. They enjoy being busy, and like to fill their days with activities that have a specific purpose. Those whose health restricts them from doing what they would like, or as much as they would like, are somewhat frustrated and feel the days are "empty," "too long," or "no good." Activity and productivity are also seen as intrinsically worthwhile; like education, they are value-laden factors.

I asked people to describe a typical day for me. Their responses illustrate the range of activities pursued and emphasize the value this group places on daily activity. The two following examples are representative in terms of the kinds of activities that constitute the daily routine. They illustrate the two dominant attitudes in the study group toward that routine. The first is a man who does as he pleases, is not limited by his health, and loves his lifestyle; the second is a woman whose choices are quite restricted by her failing health, and who is bored.

A 78-year-old man, in excellent health, spends his time as he desires. He lives with his wife, whose health is not as good as his and who is therefore less active, but this does not seem to impinge upon him or influence his decisions too much. He says:

I awaken about seven o'clock and put on the earphones
and listen to the news. I get up before eight and take a
shower and shave and dress. Then come downstairs
and get the paper, and get breakfast ready for my wife
and myself. Read the news. After breakfast I clean
up a little bit, then I usually come up here and putter
around this desk, write letters, do a little research.
I check the mail, and try to be through here around
noon. Then we have lunch. In the afternoon we usually
go out—might go downtown, might go to the park. Occasionally visit somebody. Do the shopping. Go home
about five o'clock and make a fire. Then turn on the
news about six and finish 'bout eight. Have a couple of
cocktails while we watch the news. Then get the dinner ready, and we have a nice dinner. After that, there
might be a TV program, somebody might come over.
Or we might go out to dinner with friends like we did
last night. . . . In the week, we'll also garden and do
other things. I have a full day. I don't have any time
when I sit down and say, "What do I do next?"

An 81-year-old woman has her own small apartment in a retirement residence. Her poor health limits her opportunities greatly. She feels isolated and is frustrated by the restrictions her fragility imposes upon her. She describes her day:

It's very difficult to get up in the morning because of
this emphysema and heart condition. So I make myself
get out of bed, try to make it at 6:30. I'll use the bath-
room and dress. Sitting down every five minutes it
seems to me to catch my breath. Then I go down to
breakfast, try not to talk, begin to feel I'm catching my
breath. I come upstairs about eight and read the paper.
After the paper I get up and empty my wastepaper bas-

ket, maybe make a phone call. Then do a little studying, reading. And suddenly, it's lunchtime. After lunch, we gather around the mailboxes—a big event—then I come up and read the mail. By that time, I'm awfully sleepy and I take a nap. This brings me to about 3:30. So . . . I can sit and look out the window for a long time. I'll read a little bit, file my nails, take a walk if the weather's good. Yesterday, I had my hair done. Or there's doctor appointments. We change clothes for dinner. We like it. It's a pleasant aspect. I'll meet someone for dinner downstairs, 5:15. I like an early dinner. After, generally, I come up and watch the news, take my bath and settle down to reading—light junk so you don't get too tense (laughs). Now there's a day for you. No good. Boring. I'll fill it with anything I can that keeps me busy. . . . I'm going to have to give up my car soon because my eyes are so bad. It's the illusion of independence I feel I'm giving up. . . . It's a terrible ending to live so long without having something specific to do, or being needed.

Reading, television, the household chores, walking, socializing—these are events around which many of these people's days are structured. What people do, the content of the activities themselves, does not determine the meaningfulness of daily life. Rather, the determining factor seems to be the sense of being able to choose to do what one wants. In late life, health is a key factor that can impinge on the range of choice available to the individual and, hence, on the meaning drawn from daily activity.

Family ties are another important source of meaning for my informants. Family members, especially children and grandchildren, are the primary givers of emotional support, financial aid, and household help. But above and beyond the support network function, children and grandchildren are the closest friends for the majority of these people. Some people have helped raise grandchildren for a number of years and have strong emotional bonds with their grandchildren at present. Remarks which express these close relationships include: "I'd rather be around my grandchildren than other people. They are more fun to be with"; and "I enjoy the company of my grandchildren. I feel akin to them." A few people without family say they have no close friends, and they feel a gap in their lives owing to the absence of intimate relationships.

Since family members currently provide the most intimacy and support for this group, friends play a different role, largely that of companion. Friends are those who share lifestyle and interests, whether professional or recreational. About one-quarter of the group mention long-term business associates or professional colleagues as closest friends. Most people have at least one close friend from high school, college, or the young adulthood period in general. Many have close friends from participating over the years in clubs, church groups, or community organizations. For all informants, "close" friends are those one has known and shared life experiences with for at least 20 years.

Current friendship patterns in this group are determined primarily by geographic mobility and age. About half the people interviewed have resided in this urban metropolitan area since their young adulthood. Most of them have a few "lifelong friends" who have lived in this area for most of their lives as well. Because both the research participants and the people they know have been mobile, they have made friends in different places over the years; these are now dispersed widely across the country. Many people correspond with old friends and take trips to visit them occasionally. A few people bemoan the fact that they have no close friends living nearby, or that old friends have moved away recently and it is too difficult to maintain intimate long-distance relationships.

Age affects friendship patterns in two ways. Quite a few

people mention the fact that they have outlived many or most of their friends, and this saddens them greatly. All of those who discuss friendship state that one does not make close friends when one is old. They feel that friendships depend upon building a life together, looking forward to the future and sharing expectations. When one is old, there is no future, few expectations, and thus no basis for the creation of friendships. An 81-year-old woman summarized the feelings of many on this subject when she explained to me:

> . . . The friends I've made recently I consider very
> much on the surface. When you're older you don't go
> deep into friendship. You aren't relying on them in the
> sense that you did at 35 or 40. . . . What do you hear
> from any of us? My family, my children, my grand-
> children—that's all you hear. You have no place to grow
> together. When you're younger you do. You're educating
> your children, having a social life with your husband.
> . . . When you're older, you've heard it all before . . .
> and anyway, what more is there to say?

About half of my informants specifically express satisfaction with both the number of friends they have now and the degree of closeness in those relationships. Another quarter state that they miss or need a close relationship with one person—a best friend. An 82-year-old widow summarized the view of others when she stated to me: "I know lots of people and I like them all. But I wish there was someone who lived nearby—a neighbor—for sharing and support."

Age has also affected these people's perceptions of the future. My informants share some areas of concern about possible future losses in areas that are meaningful to them now. Many people fear senility, or loss of their mental faculties, above all else. Many worry about losing their independence—"not to be able to drive a car, or something like that"—and becoming dependent on others to meet their daily needs. A few people fear the death of a spouse before their own; some others worry about the health of children or grandchildren. Several people mention inflation as their greatest present fear; they worry that the cost of living will deplete their savings before they die. A few people are most concerned about the economic and political developments in the country rather than any personal or familial state of affairs.

When I asked, "What do you look forward to now?" the answer I received, almost without exception, was some variation of this: "There is nothing to look forward to now. I just live from day to day." Many people say they have done all they wanted to do in life; they have no unfinished business, no burning desire to do more. A 70-year-old man summarizes the attitude of most people toward the future: "I don't have a plan to *become* anything now. I can't at my age. I just don't think in those terms." And the comments about the future from a 92-year-old woman typify others. "I don't want to live much longer. It seems that I've had the best that life can give me, already. What else could it give me? I mean, you enjoy your grandchildren. You see their successes. But that's not your own life." An 80-year-old woman says: "This is the end of the line, the finish. But what worries me is that it could go on a lot longer than I think." Although the ages in this study group span 27 years, from 70 to 97, the vast majority, even those in their early 70s, do not think in terms of the future, do not make long-range plans, and assume their own future to be short. The future is not perceived as a source of meaning.

The 60 members of this study group share a number of priorities with others of their age cohort across the United States. The dominant values of activity and productivity, the overwhelming importance of close family ties as well as friendships, the reliance on good health, and now, in old age, the concern with the depletion of one's life savings and the fear of senility and dependence are all commonly held attitudes among people of this age group. In other respects, these 60 people do not represent their cohort, but instead hold views shared by other urban Californians, regardless of age. Perhaps the most striking trait held by these 60 people is the acceptance of social innovation as a fact of life. With relatively little emotional or intellectual difficulty, this study group accepts the existence of the values, philosophies, and lifestyles that are continuously emerging from the California milieu. Moreover, in many cases, they are eager to study and "try out" the beliefs and practices that keep appearing in urban West Coast life.

True, the impact of behavioral experimentation, in terms of shaping the life course, is much more profound on younger people who have critical choices to make about the direction of their lives in the years ahead. But though the members of this study group are over 70, they are not unaffected by what they see happening around them. For example, the holistic health movement of the 1970s has had an impact, in some cases quite dramatic, on participants in this research. Some of them practice yoga and t'ai chi for exercise and health. Some have decided to treat their aches and pains with massage, acupuncture, and biofeedback. They are influenced, too, by the appearance of the many religious practices and sects that spring up on the West Coast. Many of my informants want to know more about the nature of Eastern religions and esoteric philosophies, and they pursue their curiosity in formal study through university extension courses and lectures, organized "retreats," or informal discussions with peers, family, and younger people.

These study participants accept the existence of passing trends, feel comfortable asking and learning about them, and are willing to seek out and embrace some of the new philosophies and practices they encounter. One reason for their awareness of and openness to these innovations lies in the fact that they see their grandchildren, and younger people generally, caught up in them. Unlike most parents of teenagers and young adults, my informants are able to be concerned, intrigued, and curious without being unduly critical. Besides possessing a general desire to keep abreast of current social trends, my informants want to find out what attracts young people to them. There is also another motive: members of this study group are willing to discuss, participate, and experiment because, just maybe, there is something positive to be gleaned from these fads and movements for their own lives. Although past social trends they have experienced are not important sources of meaning now, many of these people express their current search for meaning by an interest in current social trends.

What does an analysis of structural factors in the life story tell us about the dynamic relationship between self and culture? In the shared experience of this study group, certain structural factors are, generally speaking, more meaningful than others: they represent the conditions that these people with a common cultural background have all responded to. But within that shared framework, the content and intensity of meaning drawn from a given factor by an individual are highly idiosyncratic. To one person, a particular factor such as education may be no more than the background for more meaningful experiences; to another, it may emerge directly as an important source of meaning around which identity is constructed and themes are revealed. Thus the relationship between the structural factor and identity can be fully understood only in the framework of the individual life. We cannot generalize about a given factor's contribution to identity for a whole group, even though its members share a common cultural background.

Four

Values as Sources of Meaning

Values identify shared standards and ideals and thus represent, along with structural factors, the raw material for themes. The themes communicated by Millie, Ben, Stella, and the other informants reflect individual expressions of widely held ideals of human behavior. Shared values among the study group result from my informants' participation in a particular American experience with a specific set of symbolic goals and standards.

Values are highly abstract constructs drawn from the experiences of living in a particular society during a certain historical period. Values emerge from, and in turn are shaped by, the interactions among individuals and institutions in a social system. Clyde Kluckhohn (1951), Florence Kluckhohn (1953), Robin Williams (1970), and other social scientists have defined values as guidelines for behavior and standards by which goals are chosen and decisions are made. Kluckhohn and Strodtbeck (1961) emphasize that values are criteria which give order and direction to ongoing actions as these actions relate to solving "common human" problems. In addition, values provide a means of weighing and choosing solutions to everyday problems posed by living in a society and confronting adaptive dilemmas that occur over the life span. They also help give direction to behavior in situations of conflict and choice and lend justification to already performed action. In the preceding case illustrations, we have seen how themes function similarly to evaluate experience, guide decision-making, and explain choices. How, then, are the concepts of value and theme to be operationally distinguished from one another?

The difference between *themes* and *values* is to be found in the information they convey about the subjects. *Themes* identify the personal, idiosyncratic ways of experiencing and communicating meaning in the individual life—the ways in which people interpret experience so as to give unique internal continuity and structure to the self. Themes are based on tacit cultural assumptions about what is acceptable, but these assumptions merely provide the background for the explanation of uniqueness. *Values,* on the other hand, emphasize the individual's conformity to shared and fairly explicit indices of social worth. As such, values clearly fix the individual in a historical-cultural cohort, that is, in a group with common ideals derived from common experiences.[1]

There is more consensus in the social science literature on how values function in any given society than on the development of a list of discrete values, "value systems," or "value-orientations" for a cultural group. In his discussion of American national character, for example, the anthropologist Francis Hsu (1972) reviews much of the literature on values and describes the difficulties, contradictions, and ultimate lack of explanatory power inherent in cataloging particular values and classifying them at different levels of abstraction. I mention this problem because I have selected a number of values to highlight in this chapter. They are achievement, success, productivity, work, progress, social usefulness, independence, self-reliance, and individual initiative.

I do not claim to have identified a complete set of values for this study group. Neither am I concerned with ranking the importance of these values nor reconciling any inconsistencies among them. Rather, I have chosen to discuss these values for three reasons. First, numerous observers of American culture[2] have described them as characteristic of American society. Second, these values are shared, though to different degrees, by all research participants. Third, my analysis of the case material reveals that these values have the strongest influence on the formation of my informants' themes. These values are not necessarily "general" or "modal" American values. Rather, I want to emphasize that they characterize the participants in this study—a group of elderly, West Coast, urban, white, middle-class people.

Achievement—the attainment of a goal which brings satisfaction and heightens self-esteem—is probably a universal objective. For my informants, achievement is marked by singular, personal success in some concrete endeavor, whether it be the creation of a visible object, the ability to perform a task adequately, or the acknowledgment of one's expertise by others. An achievement is the result of some tangible behavior, purposefully enacted.

Achievement and success are to be reached through productive activity, especially work. It is not enough for these study participants to "keep busy"; their behavior must be oriented toward some pragmatic end in order to have meaning. In their study of American values, the anthropologists Conrad Arensberg and Arthur Niehoff (1975) note that in the United States a person is judged by his or her work, by his or her ability to earn a living, to contribute to the welfare of community life, or to "get ahead" in his or her occupation. Moreover, in this society the tendency is to describe a person's identity primarily in terms of his or her work role. For my informants, self-esteem is intimately related to activity and productivity, though as we have seen, the work role per se is not considered meaningful by all informants. In general, they state that their morale is highest when they feel they are working diligently and being as productive as possible. Characterizing himself at different life stages, Matthew, age 83, expresses his primary theme—*the necessity of doing work.*

> As a child, I was a dreamer; as a youth, a seeker; then I was ambitious—a doer. I don't care what, but a doer. I'm still a doer. I've never gotten out of wanting to be doing work all the time. I believe that it's your God-given duty to do something, to accomplish something. No matter what. That's it.

Matthew's earliest memory is of the poverty his family experienced. He grew up on a farm in central California, the youngest of three children, the only son. Born in 1895, he recalls the drought years at the turn of the century: "It was very bad times for everyone in the farming business. Misery, poverty were not looked down upon because everyone was poor. I had a feeling of sadness about it." In 1902, Matthew's father bought his own land, and the family's economic condition began to improve.

Matthew worked hard on the farm from the time he was seven. He had chores to do before and after school, and in the summertime he worked all day.

> As a boy, my job was called a "net jerker" on the header wagon. In those days, they were all drawn by horses. The driver of the wagon would pull up a net and hook on a cable or a rope, and my job was to get the horse to pull this off and dump it. I had to stay out there from eight in the morning to five at night. I would probably pull a load off every half hour. But I had to stay out in the field alone. I enjoyed it.

When Matthew was 15, his father died of pneumonia. The death was a terrible ordeal for the close-knit family, and Matthew missed his father a great deal in the next few years. By this time, his sisters were grown and gone from home; Matthew was left as the main support of his mother. He talks about the years following his father's death in terms of his responsibilities on the farm.

> We had about 350 acres that we farmed in barley and hay. When my father died, in the winter time, I would have to get up and harness the horses, feed them, at four in the morning. Then I'd come in and have breakfast. Then I'd have to milk the cows and do the ploughing. Then go to school. In the summertime, I'd mow the barley and hay with a mowing machine and rake it. I worked very hard.

At the insistence of his mother and with the financial aid of one of his sisters, who was a nurse, Matthew entered the university at 18. He studied philosophy and made ends meet by washing dishes and waiting on tables. He says he always had an inferiority complex regarding his intellectual capabilities. Though he was a good student, he stressed to me that he was "never a star" and was not the studious reader he might have been. World War I began during his third year, and it became the most pressing concern in his life during his last two years at the university. A month before graduation, he joined the American Field Ambulance Service—the United States had not yet declared war—and went off to Europe with a group of other young men to aid the British. To this day, Matthew feels guilty that he was handed his diploma without having to take his final examinations.

Matthew spent the war years in Europe, first as an ambulance driver, then in the army. When the war ended, he married an English woman and became a travel agent, organizing tours for Americans and traveling all over Europe. He enjoyed those years tremendously. When he was not touring, he lived with his wife and three children in England. When the depression struck, his business declined drastically. Finally, in 1935, with the rise of Hitler and at the urging of his in-laws, he returned to the United States with his wife and children. Matthew arrived in New York with his family, $28, and no prospect of a job. He was 40 years old. He says of that time:

> That was the lowest ebb of my life. I thought I was going to have a nervous breakdown. I would wake up in the middle of the night, crying. I had too much pride, but I had to ask my mother, who was still alive then, for $100 to rent a couple of rooms and get started looking for a job.

After several miserable months, he got his break. Americans were starting to travel once more to Europe, and Matthew met a travel agent who wanted him to open an office on the West Coast. He moved his family back to California, set up an office, and was immediately successful. He told me, "I did so well in the first four or five months, they couldn't believe it in the New York office." Through his foresight and hard work, the business expanded and diversified. Matthew became a vice president and stayed with the company until he retired at age 65.

Now 83, Matthew looks 10 or 15 years younger and is extremely agile for his age. Since his retirement, he and his wife have traveled extensively in the United States and around the world. When at home, he enjoys gardening and playing energetically with his small grandchildren. He also attends to many household chores himself. During the period of our interviews, he was replacing all the rotten window frames in his home with new ones. His primary theme remains important in his old age: he says his greatest wish at present is to do more work than he has time to do.

The details of his life story are unique, but Matthew's theme, the necessity of doing work, is similar to certain themes of other research participants because it reflects shared value-orientations. Matthew shares certain experiences with others in the study group as well. For example: the early experience of poverty and the drive to overcome it by hard work; the responsibility, from a young age, of contributing to the family welfare; parents who believed that education was the means to financial reward and heightened self-esteem; the opportunity for occupational mobility— all of these were pivotal experiences for many informants. Taken together, these structural factors interacted with the values of achievement, productivity, and success in informants' lives. As sources of meaning, they have emerged as themes for many members of this study group.

Activity directed toward the attainment of specific goals and personal accomplishments underscores commitment to the concept of progress. Arensberg and Niehoff (1975) and Williams (1970) describe the American view of progress as faith in the future of changing institutions and the development of technology. My informants tend to see progress as follows: they strive for occupational success and perfection in the tasks they undertake, and they work on character development, for example, "overcoming my shyness," "getting out and being with people more often," "seeing something worthwhile in everyone," and "trying to be more patient with others." All study group members believe that, with personal effort, their temperaments can be improved, their material lives enriched, and their work be made more gratifying.

In a society where progress is assumed to be possible and activity is directed toward solving problems, humanitarian behavior, too, is evaluated in the context of performance and achievement. For example, service to community organizations, philanthropy through formal institutions, and personal acts of generosity are all pragmatic expressions of concern for others that can be measured and judged. For this study group, such behavior is defined as socially useful. That is, giving time or money to others is viewed in terms of both the *results* it will bring to the larger community and the *contribution* being made by the individual.

Bess, at 82, puts her philosophy of life in a nutshell: "Do the best you can. Give a little, take a little." She describes much of her life through the theme, *dedication to community service*, and she structures her account around the philanthropic committees on which she has served over the years, her abilities as an organizer and civic leader, and her effectiveness in providing services and raising money.

Bess immigrated to the United States with her well-to-do family from Czechoslovakia in 1908. She was 12 at the time. The oldest of three children and the only girl, she says she was used to getting what she wanted and has always been stubborn, headstrong, and rebellious. Bess told me that when her family arrived in New York, her mother wanted her to retain her upper-class European lifestyle and arranged for Bess to be tutored privately at home. But Bess insisted on learning English as quickly as possible and entering the public schools. Later, her mother wanted her to become a lawyer; Bess rejected that idea and took accounting, typing, sewing, and cooking classes in school.

The family moved from New York to the West Coast in 1911 when Bess's father, an inventor, decided to go into business with an uncle. When Bess finished high school, she went to work as an accountant for a manufacturing company, much to her mother's dismay, as she did not need to work. A few years later, when World War I began and the company for which Bess worked turned exclusively to war production, Bess changed jobs, noting that, at 18, with her skills and the war on, she was in great demand and could have whatever job she chose.

Bess met her husband during the war years; when the war ended, her husband-to-be was just starting an electronics company. Bess quit her job the week before the wedding and went to work as the accountant for her husband's company. Reflecting on her past, Bess says her husband was the most influential person in her life, and the only person she ever wanted to please. "He toned me down. I always did what he wanted me to do." He would never let her work for a salary, even during the early years of their marriage when they could have used the money. But, as his business became more successful and they became quite affluent, he encouraged her to do philanthropic work.

Much of Bess's account is devoted to describing her work with the Red Cross and army during World War II. Though she worked long hours, she relished the work she did in those years and apparently placed herself in charge of whatever project she was engaged in at the time. On different occasions, she organized housing, food distribution, and entertainment for the hundreds of soldiers who were stationed in this urban metropolitan area on their way to or from the South Pacific. Bess talks about her "war work" in terms of her effectiveness in getting things done her way and her ability to organize other people in order to accomplish some task. "Every week I would get together with the special service officers of the army and navy to provide entertainment, and I had to allocate the talent to be fair to each place. Then I had to organize units to send out the entertainers. . . ." Beginning with her service during the war years, Bess portrays herself as influential and powerful in the community and is quite proud of these characteristics.

When the war was over, Bess became actively involved in civic and church groups. She devoted the next 40 years to fund-raising for numerous local, national, and international organizations, serving on many boards and committees, and acting as the "hostess with the mostest" by offering her large and beautiful home for fund-raising events, meetings, and gatherings of all kinds.

Now, Bess describes herself as a semi-invalid. When I

asked her to describe the hardest thing about growing old, she replied:

> I just wish I could get the hell out and do more things. I still belong to 27 organizations. But I just send them checks now. I'm not very active anymore. . . . I wish I could be like my friend F. B. You should see her— 90 years old, but she's always running around, never misses a meeting.

Bess's self-image and sense of worth in the world derive from her lifelong community affiliations and sense of serving others. Now, with various medical problems, she can no longer be involved in her community as she would like—by being a leader and giving her time and energy to others. Moreover, she can no longer maintain the active social life which has always accompanied her philanthropic endeavors. This is a great frustration to her.

Bess's sense of self and the structure of her life course are interpreted in a framework of social usefulness. Her life story emphasizes humanitarian behavior more than others I collected, yet it is not highly unusual; Bess rebelled against her upper-class, socially insulated background as did some other study participants. Most informants, however, were socialized by their mothers—regardless of religion or class—to regard humanitarian behavior as the most valued activity. We recall that informants remember their mothers as "devoted," "charitable," "good," "giving," "kind." By setting an example, mostly through church and community work, the mothers taught these people to give of themselves to others— and to do so with sincerity and integrity—as they went through life. Now, at the end of their lives, informants continue to place high value on social usefulness and to judge their lives in terms of it.

In American society generally, the values of achievement, productivity, work, progress, and social usefulness accentu-

ate the autonomy and worth of the individual. For my informants, individualism is expressed primarily in three ideal
character traits. The first is independence, the ability to provide for one's own physical and emotional needs. The more
frail and infirm study participants, while realistically ac-
knowledging their partial dependence on others, also hold
this ideal. They attempt to be as autonomous as they can,
considering their specific health needs, and they exert much
energy to avoid being "a burden," "an inconvenience," or a
"third wheel."

The second trait that contributes to individualism is self-
reliance. The anthropologist Hsu (1972:250) defines it:
". . . under this ideal every individual is his own master, in
control of his own destiny, and will advance and regress in
society only according to his own efforts." To this statement
I would add the notion of self-determination: with enough
personal intention and effort, almost all obstacles can be
overcome, the environment can be manipulated, and one can
improve oneself.

The third expression of individualism in the data I collected is initiative. These people not only stress the need for
firm resolve and personal responsibility in action, they also
emphasize the importance of taking the first step in an endeavor. They maintain a feeling that nobody else can, or
should, do things for them and that they must create their
own successes, from scratch.

Industry and *initiative* are two themes that emerge in
Arthur's account. Determined from a young age to make
something of himself, Arthur began to work when he was 12,
after school. A neighbor owned a candy factory, and Arthur
used to help him both in the factory and by selling candies,
fruits, and spices to grocery stores and to housewives in his
neighborhood. He discovered he loved selling. "I was an aggressive youngster. I wanted to get somewhere. I was always
seeking ways of making money. I loved selling. I loved the
work, and that stayed with me through the years."

Arthur was born in 1886 in a West Coast city. His parents were comfortable financially; his father was an accountant and his mother was a schoolteacher. Arthur had a middle-class childhood: he went to the public schools, joined the boy scouts, and had no financial obligations. Yet, he was driven to be independent, and he enjoyed working toward his goal. In 1903, when he graduated from high school, he went to see an acquaintance who owned a small spice and flavoring company.

> I went to see him and said, "I was told you need a salesman." He said, "Yes," and I said, "Well, I'm your man." We talked a bit, and he said, "How much salary do you want?" I said, "I don't want a salary; I want a job." So he put me down for $100 a month. And he gave me a badly written price list and price book and said, "You'll cover the entire territory which is 10 states." So I started in Reno, Nevada, and went on from there to Ogden, Utah, and Salt Lake City. I did quite a job selling in those places. When I got to Salt Lake, I got a wire from the boss: "Salary now $150—keep going." So from there I went to Boise, Idaho, and up into Montana and across the mountain states to Seattle and covered all the territory in between. . . .

In 1907, with a partner, Arthur started his own wholesale food business. He was the salesman and the secretary for the company. Business grew rapidly. Arthur married and had three children. Over the years, his company expanded; he bought out a manufacturing firm, then a restaurant chain. Arthur was sales manager, "chasing 14 salesmen around the country," and then vice president. He loved all aspects of his work and is extremely proud of the business he built. He summarizes his career: "I started as the only salesman in the company. It grew to a tremendous size. We did a $4 million business, starting from scratch."

When Arthur was 75, his doctor told him to slow down, so reluctantly, he reduced his time at work. At age 78, he finally retired, but only at the urging of both his wife and doctor. Now 92, Arthur says he enjoyed sales so much because he has always liked being around people. His business associates and some of his customers became his closest friends over the years. He feels he was successful because he has always been able to find something good in everyone he meets, and because he has always been honest in his business dealings. When I asked Arthur who were the most influential people in his life, he mentioned, first, his mother, who taught him to live by the Golden Rule—"that's the only religion I ever had." He then named three individuals, each of whom gave him the opportunity for further independence in his career and "the assurance that I was going to go places." He concluded by saying: "But nobody contributed to my successes in any great measure. I've always been my own man. I've always felt that I had to do things on my own, and I did."

The values which gave shape to Arthur's life remain with him in old age. He channeled his early desire to shape his own fate into sales work. With untiring ambition and initiative, he built up a successful business. Self-reliant throughout life, he insists on retaining his autonomy now. The maintenance of independence in old age is crucial to the emotional well-being of all study participants, because, like Arthur, they too have spent a lifetime expressing individualism in purposeful activity. The value of independence, having helped shape the life course, is rarely discarded as useless when a person becomes old. Rather, it continues to provide guidelines for behavior, to serve as an index of social worth, and to be part of the foundation on which identity is built.

These values—achievement, productivity, progress, social usefulness, individualism—derive from the shared cultural background and historical period in which my informants have lived. Taken together, these values provide meaning as a source of self-expression.

In her study of aging and American values, Margaret Clark (1967; 1972; [Clark and Anderson] 1967) found that methods of realizing certain dominant American values differed among a mentally well group of older people and a mentally ill group.

Persons who rigidly cling to such values as individualism, competitiveness, aggressiveness, achievement, and future-orientation in their old age, for example, are good candidates for geriatric psychiatry. On the other hand, individuals who show flexibility in substituting conservation for acquisition, cooperation for competition, and coexistence for control, for instance, appear mentally healthy in old age. Clark concludes that people must either bring a broad and flexible spectrum of value-orientations into old age, or they must be able to change their values markedly once they reach old age in order for adaptation to occur. Her point is to illustrate how the elderly are victims of a profound cultural discontinuity: values they have held throughout life are no longer appropriate in old age.

Though not addressing the adaptive/maladaptive issue directly, my discussion extends that of Clark. While her work focuses on the need for individuals to alter their orientations to face the contradiction between dominant values and the limitations of old age, I explore the ways in which old people are willing and able to reinterpret their experience so that old values take on new meaning appropriate to present circumstances. Clark stresses that changes demanded of old people represent cultural discontinuity. I emphasize ways in which old people formulate their identities to create symbolic continuity. The process of reinterpretation I describe *is* highly adaptive: through it, individuals create a coherent picture of their pasts and a purposeful, integrated present.

The following three case studies illustrate how values are interpreted in the life story, how they appear to have evolved over the life course, and how they are maintained into old age.

Mary

Mary, 72 years old, evaluates her life and recalls past experiences in the framework of a *wasteful-productive dichotomy,* a dominant theme in her life story. Her identity apparently has been shaped largely by the way she defines productiveness and the value she attaches to it. Productiveness is any tangible, "marketable skill" that can be channeled into a specific job or task and which leads to a clearly stated goal or profession. She considers the absence or lack of application of such skills to be wasteful. Mary creates her account around the depiction of events which are conceived to have hindered or promoted her progress in obtaining a profession and her own lack of ability and initiative to reach this goal. Over and over, she makes such remarks as: "I wasted myself for many years, 20 years or so. I had never trained to do anything . . . and I just drifted along. I went through a long period where I didn't care for myself. I was suffering a sort of shame of not really being anything."

A factor which Mary feels contributed to her nonproductive sense of self was her general liberal arts college education, which she thoroughly enjoyed but which left her unprepared professionally and with a feeling of having failed. She looks back on that period as having missed a great opportunity—to take a teacher-training course and become a teacher in a small midwestern town, thus gaining self-esteem and a profession. She says: "But I didn't want to be trained to be a teacher. I don't think I have it in me to be a good teacher. That was a sort of stop-gap anyway. What was I going to do? That was the only thing I could do, seemingly." She felt that the lifestyle apparently required by that professional choice—living with members of the school board,

teaching Sunday school, and following strict behavior guidelines—was too repressive and dull for her. She explains: "By
that time I had encountered Culture. I was mad about drawing. I had painter friends and musician friends. I had evenings listening to Stravinsky and Scriabin, drinking wine.
We went to the museums. I couldn't even think of leaving
the city; it just killed me. So I bowed out completely." In retrospect, she regrets that decision. "I didn't have the confidence to do it. I was afraid. And that was a serious error on
my part and contributed to my sense of failure. I had refused
a test actually." Later in our discussions, when I asked if
there was anything she would do differently given the chance
to relive her life, she unhesitatingly said she would take that
small-town teaching position.

Mary views the sequence of events in her middle years as
reinforcing the sense of waste in her life. Instead of teaching
after college, she took a "terribly dull" clerical job which
she held for several years, until her marriage in 1930. During
the early years of her marriage, she and her husband moved
around the country quite a bit as he went from job to job,
and their moves, coupled with the fact that those years were
the height of the depression, are the reason she now gives for
never establishing herself in a career at that time. Later on,
she was raising her children, and while they were young she
did not dwell too much on her "lack of skills" or "wasted
time."

Mary's critical turning point came when she was 50; her
husband left her. She says the biggest shock of that event
was the realization that she would have to support herself financially, and she feared "ending up scrubbing floors." After
much deliberation and some encouragement from a friend,
she decided to go back to school and become a librarian. She
now views this choice as her biggest step toward productiveness, and says, "At last I had gotten up the nerve to prepare
to do something." She defines completing her training and

acquiring her first job as the high points in her life. She told me: "I loved the campus, I loved the study, I loved the work. It did a terrific thing for me. I felt as if I'd taken a proper direction. I really felt like something. Now, I had a function." For the first time in her life, Mary felt a sense of personal worth. She had a purpose in the world—she was working, she had a clearly defined role, and she was engaging in what she regarded as meaningful, productive activity. She claims that her self-image has steadily improved over the years since she made the decision to become a librarian and that she has "made more friends and had more fun" than ever before. Her ability to be productive, as she defines it, has made the last 20 years of her life the best by far.

Through a second theme, Mary gauges her experiences over the years by whether or not they have contributed to or detracted from her self-confidence. She does this by plotting out her memories along a *life span – confidence continuum:* moving from no self-confidence as she rejected the small-town teaching job, to the gradual acquisition of confidence in her middle years, to her strong sense of who she is in the world now. Through this theme she explains the turnings, the patterns of adaptation, and the sequence of events in her life. For Mary, the building of confidence in her lifetime is the expression of both progress and achievement.

Mary describes herself during her youth and young adulthood as "terribly shy and scared." She feels she could not take the teaching job because of a "lack of self-determination." She defines her lack of confidence as a "source of uneasiness until my mid-40s." When she was 45, she and her family moved to a small town where she met a couple who had a profound influence on her life. They took an active role in the development of her self-esteem by providing her much emotional support, something no one had attended to previously.

She was an only child in a household beset by constant financial difficulties and worries. She spent much time alone and remembers her father as an aloof, distant man and her mother as a preoccupied, bitter woman. As she tells it, when she was a small child, her father invested and subsequently lost stock that her mother had inherited. Until then, the family had lived in a beautiful home and lovely neighborhood. Mary dimly recalls her mother dressed in exquisite satin dresses, playing the piano. When the money was lost, the family had to move to "the wrong side of the tracks," and her mother went to work in the local factory—a big step downward in status for them all. Mary says that her mother felt her father had ruined her life; the parents barely spoke with each other from that time onward, and there was much unresolved tension in the air. In addition, Mary's parents never paid much attention to her. She has strong memories of being dismissed from the room whenever she came in to talk with them. This was not an atmosphere in which confidence could develop easily.

During Mary's own marriage, her husband was absorbed in his work—painting—and Mary felt he did not provide her with much emotional support either. She says their biggest problem throughout the marriage was that they did not know how to communicate with one another; this was one of the major reasons for the divorce. Her children, too, contributed to her sense of uneasiness and frustration with herself. She says she had never held a baby before she had her own and felt very uncomfortable taking care of her own infants. In retrospect, she feels she did not hold them enough when they were small and did not understand what they were going through when they were older. She says, as a mother "I was such a dumb creature. I didn't know anything about it. I don't know why I didn't read more in the field; I was so inept."

In a sense, the couple whom Mary met in midlife were her first family. They openly loved and nurtured her, and she was truly comfortable in their presence. She describes what they did for her: "They were very intuitive and saw my lack of self-confidence, and they just began building me up. They showed me things, set up a reading program for me, lent me all their books, and taught me a lot. We had more fun together than I had ever had. . . . They kept reassuring me, and telling me I was good enough. . . ." She interprets this friendship as the first big step on her path to self-confidence.

A few years after she met this couple, Mary had to go to work to help support her family because her husband's career as an artist was not successful. She got a part-time job selling door-to-door, which she held for several years. Its worth is measured along the confidence continuum also. "It was a good experience. I was at last working, and it gave me more confidence." Though her marriage was deteriorating and her financial situation was unstable, she felt better about her life than ever before because she was "being productive." Then came her divorce and her training to become a librarian, which raised her self-esteem to an even higher level.

Numerous observers of the American scene have noted that the values of productivity, progress, and achievement were dominant in this society at least through the period of World War II, when Mary and the other members of this study group were growing up and in their prime. Since values, once given shape in the individual life, are not modified easily, they remain with the individual into old age and function as a source for identity formulation. And values do work in that way to shape Mary's themes and those of the other informants.

For the present, *observer of life* supplements the *wasteful-productive dichotomy* theme and offers a new interpretation of productiveness. Mary expresses this theme in a beautiful metaphor when she describes what the 72 years of her life have been about:

> I just say I've been wandering through a meadow, sampling, enjoying as I went. . . . I get so much pleasure and amusement in watching people and observing the world around me—the things that happen, the fleeting moment when something is revealed is really quite funny, or pathetic. I mean I feel surrounded by a lot of visual and verbal dramas that are not valued for what they are by the people who are in them.

The "wandering" and "sampling" of the theme are alternatives to the "drifting" in the wasteful-productive dichotomy. In that theme, "drifting" is negative—behavior that has no purpose, no goal. "Sampling" implies a freedom to engage in any activity one chooses, to pursue variety, to experience much. It is Mary's positive accounting of the path her life has taken. As she equates "drifting along" with wastefulness, so she evaluates her "wanderings" as fruitful, because they led her to a deeper understanding of humanity; they were also productive. The two themes coexist in her life story.

From the biographical context of these two themes, I would venture to hypothesize that the wasteful-productive dichotomy has been an explanation of experience for a long time. It is a direct expression of a cultural norm during Mary's youth and middle adulthood, and Mary employs it to talk about herself over the years. In contrast, her observer-of-life theme seems to have emerged with the knowledge of hindsight and the experience of many years; it gives new meaning to productiveness in late life.

Mary's self-acceptance was clearly evident when I asked, "What is the hardest thing about growing older?" She thought carefully and then replied: "Well, truly, I am happier now than I've ever been, I think. Certainly more adjusted. I think this is a sort of high point in my life. I believe I'm being realistic." The observer-of-life theme is a positive evaluation of lifelong behavior patterns. This theme also integrates Mary's perception of the "wasteful" years with her current acceptance of her life course and enjoyment of the world around her.

Harold

How values may find expression at different stages of an individual's life is well illustrated by the formulation and integration of themes in another life story. Harold, a 76-year-old retired business executive, views his entire life as a sequence of building, reaping the rewards from, and sharing economic and professional *success.*

Harold came from a poor family. His father owned a harness and buggy shop in a small town, and business was poor during Harold's childhood as more and more people bought automobiles. In 1920, when Harold was 18, the business collapsed. An only child, brought up in a religious atmosphere where heavy emphasis was placed on making a success in life and helping others, Harold felt a moral obligation to save his parents from financial disaster. There were few jobs available to him in the small town where he grew up, and none of those paid very well, so, at the suggestion of a relative in a large city, Harold moved away from his parents in order to provide for them. He feels that was the most difficult and crucial decision in his life. He was torn; he did not want to leave them, but he knew it was the only way to find a job that would enable him to support himself and send money home. That conflict set the stage for his professional motivation later. Of that time he states: "Because of what happened to my family, I became determined never to let this happen to me. I had a strong desire to attain recognition and success, and I set out to do it."

The rest of Harold's life story is constructed around his successes. Though he has a wife and three children who he claims are important to him, they hardly figure in his account. I do not know the reason for his one-sided account. Perhaps he does not feel his marriage is a success. Or perhaps he assumed that I was interested primarily in his career, not his personal life. At any rate, Harold's story, though detailed in many respects, does gloss over his family life.

Harold defines his first success as obtaining a job with a growing manufacturing company, for through it he fulfilled his moral obligation. "My first success was getting that job, because it enabled me to send money back to the family . . . and I was able to do that for the rest of their lives." From that point on, his account deals primarily with the progress and the adventures leading to success within the company where he worked for 45 years.

Harold talks at length about his early days on the job, which are vivid in his memory.

> I started off doing things I didn't know how to do. I'll never forget that one time some executive came up, and he wanted me to take a letter. I didn't know how to tell him that I didn't take shorthand or I didn't know how to type. I decided to play the thing, maybe I could remember it. But I couldn't get any of it. And he must have known, so what was I going to do now? I told him I couldn't take shorthand, but I'd learn. And I went to night school. . . . I used to stay there late at night, try to clean up my work, do the best I could to hold onto the job. . . .

When I asked him to describe himself during his 20s and 30s, he replied: "I was trying hard to make a success. By this time, I was office manager and I had the responsibility of the business. So, I was always concerned about it." His self-description of the years that followed is also in terms of building his career. "In my 40s, I was concerned about whether or not I was going to make it to the top. . . . Then I was riding on a crest, I had reached my goals." He became a vice president. The company asked him to stay on for several years after he thought of retiring, and he did. He was respected and needed by others for his work, and he knew that he had helped build the business. Besides the desire for professional success, there is another reason Harold was so totally immersed in his career: he worshiped his boss. From Harold's descriptions, their relationship seems to have fulfilled many roles—father/son, best friends, teacher/disciple, and patron/apprentice. His boss taught him the business, gave him many opportunities for advancement, bought him a home, and involved Harold in the affairs of his lively personal life, which included making whisky in a basement during Prohibition, visiting local celebrities, and giving huge, rowdy parties. Harold sums up the effect of that relationship on his life:

> Life with H. J. was very, very exciting. I had more exciting experiences with him at work than you can possibly believe. And this is one of the things that contributed much to my life, I'm sure. The average person goes through life without the excitement, the achievements that were possible because of H. J.

Harold must continue being successful in retirement, and he has found a way to do so by "sharing" his success with others as a member of a volunteer organization which advises small businesses. He says: "We're all retired, from successful businesses. And we just have a bulk of knowledge. People with small businesses come to us and we counsel them about a problem, or an idea for expansion, or if they're having difficulties with their loan payments." He views this work as giving others the chance for a successful life. As he has been motivated to achieve success throughout his life, he tries to motivate others now.

Harold claims his road to success has been via salesmanship. He worked his way to prominence in business as a salesman, and now, as well as in retrospect, he sees himself as a *salesman* in all contexts, social as well as business. Through this second theme, he structures encounters so that he is the "seller" and the other person is the "buyer." He perceives sales as a technique to control others' behavior and one's own destiny. He says, "You can't force anyone to anything, but I think you can sell a person most anything." He defines the nature of all activity in terms of sales. "We're all selling, regardless of what it is. We're selling something. And I think the closer you are to selling, the more your opportunities are, and the less your frustrations are."

In the course of our discussions, Harold mentioned several times that he was taught the sales technique of "obligating the merchant" in his business. He feels this technique can and should be applied to other areas of life as well in order to achieve whatever goals one has in mind. He uses this phrase to mean that in social relationships one should create a structure of reciprocal ties: if you do someone a favor, that person must return the favor by giving you what you need to get ahead. For instance, Harold feels he can use this technique to make new friends now. "The best way to get friends is to do something for them. Take them for a ride, ask them over for a drink, maybe a game of cards. You have to obligate the merchant. . . . If you have any sales ability at all, there's a million ways you can do it. . . ." And later he remarked, "You can build up a circle of acquaintances who will become good friends by doing their shopping, taking them to the senior citizen center, phoning them at night, helping them in different ways."

Besides sales techniques, a strong sense of individual initiative propelled Harold to success in his profession. From the time his father's business failed, Harold was determined to forge his own career. His story of how he worked his way up in his profession illustrates the weight he gives to the values of initiative and self-determination. He started at the age of 19 as an office boy, and he says of that period: "I went to night school, though I didn't have to, to learn typing and shorthand. I was determined to do well." As he looks back on the period when he acquired more responsibility, his image of himself is that of "pioneer." At various stages in his career, he personally instituted new technical innovations in the company, sometimes without organizational support. He is extremely proud of these innovations; he now feels that "pioneering a new thing" was the ultimate measure of his success.

In addition, Harold respects individual initiative and autonomy in other people more than any other qualities. I spent one Christmas with Harold and his family, and after the meal was finished and gifts were shared, he gathered his family and friends around him to tell "a story of Christmas—what life is all about really." With much emotion, he related the story of a man whom he met in his capacity as a volunteer small-business consultant. The man was a jeweler and, though quite competent at his craft, he was beset by problems in making a living. His store had been robbed several times, he had no knowledge of business operations, he had serious health problems, and he was extremely poor. After describing this man's personal tragedies and professional troubles in great detail, Harold said:

> S. is a perfect example of a person who comes to us for
> help and does what we tell him, and makes it work.
> He was a great jeweler but he didn't know much about
> business. I gave him all the information he needed
> to run a business. And he did it, and he's successful
> now. The remarkable thing is that he wouldn't accept

any help or welfare or charity. He insisted on doing it
all himself. I really love that man.

The story of Christmas—the embodiment of faith and all
that is good in the world—is summarized here by Harold's
faith in the jeweler and by the jeweler's incentive to pull
himself up by his own bootstraps, to remain self-sufficient in
the face of great difficulties. For Harold, initiative and self-
determination are the most valued character traits.

The value of social usefulness emerges in Harold's life
story as well. He expresses this value in the phrase, "obligating the merchant," and in doing so, he imparts new meaning
at this life stage to the themes of *success* and *salesmanship*.
In this way, he creates continuity of identity.

The importance of social usefulness as a moral imperative
emerges when Harold talks about the philosophical guiding
force in his life. He conceives of a circle of goodness in the
world; it is his responsibility to pass on to others the good
life he has received, so that there is a balance of goodness
through the world, a completion of the circle, and a sense of
closure in his own life. This notion emerged when I asked
him what plans he has made for the future and how he views
his retirement. He replied: "Those of us who have had a
pretty wonderful life owe a little bit. If there's an opportunity
to pay it back, we should. . . . I'm very anxious to help those
less fortunate so I can contribute something, pay back a little
of the wonderful things that have happened to me. What could
be better?" This view of his relationship to others is, of
course, based upon his sense of success in his own life. His
business knowledge, confidence, and financial resources all
make it possible for him to help others now.

The direct application of his professional knowledge in
the small-business consulting organization is one way he
gives his success to others. But his desire to help people is
not channeled only into business; Harold goes beyond that.

For example, he insisted on taking the jeweler who had so many health as well as business problems to his own physician, and he paid for the required medical treatments. Harold knew that in order for this man to become a success in business his health problems would have to be attended to first. And he helps a number of frail elderly, both neighbors and old friends, with household chores and errands and with getting appropriate services from government agencies. He sees himself in the role of service provider for both business novices and the infirm elderly. He has created this role since his retirement, and he currently has plans to expand his work in both areas.

In the context of Harold's perception of the past, success is defined through the professional achievements of technological inventions and increased job responsibilities. Since he is now retired, Harold has had to change that definition in order to maintain a sense of continuity. By helping others in business and contributing to *their* progress, Harold extends his own success. Through his consulting work, he has been able to help keep the jeweler and other people financially solvent, thus enabling them to maintain their own businesses. Also, Harold views his aid to his elderly friends as a way to keep them from becoming institutionalized. For example, of his behavior toward one frail neighbor he states: "I'm trying to keep her in her apartment. I've called various people, arranged for housecleaning and hot meals to be brought in. And I take her for rides and fix things in her apartment. And she calls me in the middle of the night sometimes, when fear sets in. . . ." As long as he can help this woman and other elderly people to remain independent and can improve people's business opportunities, he can consider himself successful.

Harold's themes are maintained also through his desire to be needed, which became evident when I asked him what is the most difficult thing about growing older. He answered:

"Accepting the fact that the company doesn't need you any-more. Some of us have much to offer, much to contribute, and we shouldn't be set aside." He sees himself as productive and active in the world still and resents his retirement be-cause it makes the expression of those values much more difficult. In fact, he told me that the key to well-being and peace of mind in old age was "being needed."

Though Harold is no longer needed by the professional world, he perceives himself as much needed by one of his children still living at home. His daughter, M., is a success-ful professional young woman who has a busy schedule man-aging both her small business and active social life. When I asked Harold to tell me how he spends his days now, he men-tioned, "I am a kind of general flunky for M." He sees him-self both as M.'s errand-boy and her professional advisor. He feels complimented that she takes his advice where her busi-ness is concerned, and he enjoys running small errands for her. By helping his daughter in these ways, he remains useful and escapes boredom in his daily routine. He told me, "With M., life is not dull around here." He seems to derive much pleasure living in the wake of her exciting, active life.

Harold is needed by his semi-invalid wife also, but he never discussed this aspect of his life with me. In the years that I have known him, I have observed him cooking for her, driving her wherever she wants to go, and pacing his daily schedule around her needs and energy level. He does not leave her alone in the house very often. He is devoted to her and is quite attentive. Though Harold does much for his wife, he never talked about his care-giver role as he con-structed his account. I believe this gap is due to his inter-pretation of that role: assisting his infirm wife does not con-tribute to his successful self-image as does helping others in business, providing and arranging services to other elderly, and advising his daughter. Perhaps he feels that his wife can make no *progress* as can the other people he assists. Or maybe he believes that caring for his wife, a private matter, is not a contribution to society, a symbol of productivity in the world still, as are his other service-oriented activities.

At any rate, by contributing to the welfare of business people, the frail elderly, and his daughter, Harold has created a means of continuing to feel needed and important in society. The maintenance of his salesman style of interaction accentuates his continued usefulness: by structuring relationships so that he is performing a service during the course of social interaction, he actually makes others come to depend on him for repeated aid, or at least, he is able to define the situation so that others appear to turn to him for help.

Alice

The value of work as goal-oriented, instrumental performance is given form and meaning in several themes in Alice's autobiography. In her primary theme, work is expressed as the *search for spiritual understanding.* She explains that her whole life has been oriented toward "probing," "seeking," and "finding" spiritual insight.

Alice, 81, states that from the time of her young adulthood she was motivated by "an inner craving for understanding." She observed and experimented with the practices and rituals of a variety of religions over a 15-year period in her quest for that understanding. She says that when she was in her mid-30s, "something clicked. There comes a time in life when you're ready." One evening she heard a non-Western religious group leader give a lecture, and she was extremely impressed with his presence and ideas. A few weeks later she joined his sect, and since then she has devoted her life to its service and to the acquisition of spiritual knowledge through its teachings and philosophy.

Alice claims that the drive to find something that would

explain the meaning of life was instilled by her mother at an early age. Her parents were divorced when she was three, and she remembers being very sensitive to and upset by her mother's precarious financial situation, which was caused by insufficient alimony payments from her father. She recalls her early childhood as "a bitter time," and as a "tremendous shock" for her mother. A few years after the divorce, her mother married a prominent physician whom they both adored. But because of his occupational commitments, he was not at home much, and Alice's mother became depressed and lonely. She describes her mother's behavior throughout her childhood and youth:

> She went through life seeking, seeking, seeking. We had a long hall at home; it was lined with books, and many times I'd come home from school and find her on the floor, books all around her, going through the Bible, looking, looking, looking, and crying her heart out. I'd say, "What's the matter?" And she'd say, "I'm hunting for an answer." And she made herself physically sick with her longing. . . . At the end of her life, she had a very illuminating experience, and the answer came, and it was quite beautiful.

This picture of her mother's needs clearly influenced her own. She says that during her youth she resented her mother's preoccupation with religion and philosophy and felt she was being neglected. It was not until her mother died that she joined the religious sect, and she could not understand her mother's need for spiritual satisfaction until she had sought and then found her own.

Discipline, a second theme, is the word Alice uses to characterize her approach to the work in her life. She explains that her mother raised her with a "rigid discipline"—Alice looks back on a strict, restricted upbringing where discipline was imposed upon her. Her mother also taught her self-reliance and self-control from an early age, and Alice notes that these were the dominant values of her peer group as well while she was growing up. She says about getting her first job: "That was more discipline. Six days a week. You see, from about 1915 on, those of us who were young in those days were disciplined. We just didn't skate off at the drop of a hat. We took a long time to get Saturday afternoon off. . . ."

Later, the lifestyle required by her religious sect was "quiet and disciplined." By the time she discovered this group, discipline, in the sense of both systematic diligence toward a task and self-control, was no longer only the value of others; she had established it as her key to attaining spiritual insight. She spent years studying long hours and working toward her goals of "greater perception" and "a higher level of truth." She feels that her "disciplined approach" has led her to the answers she sought about the meaning of life.

Alice approached her professional work with the same resolve as her religious strivings. She was a fashion designer, and she started her profession and built it into a thriving business, motivated by a strong sense of responsibility for her own survival and success. Her emphasis on self-reliance colors all her career descriptions. For example, she says of the time when she finished college and began looking for a job: "It wasn't a very big profession at that time, and there was a minor recession. It's just awful to go from door to door and ask for work, but I did it. I had to earn a living. And I came home so discouraged." After becoming employed and working several years for others, she started her own business in 1930. She never married and had to continue supporting herself, and she remembers being "scared, terrified" during the depression years. She describes the first decade of her career: "I just had to put one foot in front of the other and keep going. Sometimes I thought the door would have to be closed . . . but suddenly, it just seemed to march along. . . . I built up a nice clientele, got repeat business a great deal. And when you get repeat business, you know you've made good." Alice views her primary achievement not as creating a successful business, but rather as learning to cope, that is, surmounting the difficulties and overcoming the fears she faced throughout her life. Coping with her mother's religious fervor stands out as the major hardship of her childhood. She resented the time it took away from her needs as a growing girl, and she felt it ruined her family life. Her college years, though viewed as enjoyable in part, are described mainly in terms of frustrations to be dealt with.

I was studying art. But the frustration was that I couldn't draw worth two cents. It just wasn't in me at all. . . . And mathematics, it was dreadful. I suffered. I don't know how I got through those years; I just don't know how I did it. I got out of college with a degree that seemed something, but I felt terrible frustrations.

From the time she left college until her business proved successful—about a 20-year period—she was "scared to death" and "overcome with fear." Starting out during the depression was the biggest hardship to surmount. She thought she might starve, but she did not know what else to do except go ahead with her plans. Bringing religion into her life shortly after she started her business greatly allayed her fears and made it possible for her to tackle her business problems as they arose and to control her anxiety.

Discipline and self-reliance are the values which stand out now as the guiding forces of Alice's formative years. The general economic uncertainty of the depression and Alice's specific situation of being a single woman entering the job market during that period are the main strutural factors of her early life. These factors, together with the expectations of her family and peers, shaped Alice's limitations and opportunities. Her values contributed to her vision of life as a struggle, as a series of difficulties and fears to overcome, but they also were a guide to achieving success and higher spiritual truths.

For the last five years, Alice has had her own apartment in a beautiful retirement-residence complex located in an affluent neighborhood. Her attitude toward the retirement residence highlights a lifetime of anxiety created by the need to be self-reliant. She said to me: "I love it here. I have never been so free of responsibility." She views her presence in this environment as the crowning achievement in her life.

> Getting in here, where all your care is guaranteed—I'm
> very grateful and fortunate. It's a luxury. Everything
> is taken care of. . . . I do feel that all the steps in my
> life have contributed toward the fact that I have this
> well-being and security now.

Alice has always had to take care of herself. Now, for the first time in her life, the responsibility for her survival, and indeed for the quality of her life, is in the hands of others. She views this as a great relief, as security, and as the ultimate sign of having overcome the difficulties of her past. At this stage in life, she has gladly given up self-reliance and the fears which accompanied it for many years. She is no longer striving for financial stability or religious knowledge, and thus self-reliance, once valued as the means of reaching those goals, is no longer salient.

Service, another theme in Alice's life, is both the term given to her past activities in the religious sphere and an example of how the value of work is expressed in her life. Moreover, through her spiritually oriented work, Alice has found a partial answer to the question of the meaning of life. For about five years after she joined the religious sect, she wondered why she had made that choice. During those years, she was undecided about her degree of involvement in the sect and the form it should take, and her ambivalence toward her commitment caused her great inner conflict. This was alleviated when she discovered the relevance of service. "Suddenly, something happened. I felt something give in me. . . . I could be of service, I could contribute. I'm not a meditative type, and I'm not the student type. Service was my thing." Her service took the form of the daily administration of the affairs of the sect's temple, a center for seminars, lectures, prayer groups, and other activities. It enabled her to "be something a little higher," that is, to come closer to her goal of insight.

The search for spiritual understanding is no longer a major force in her life. Nevertheless, service remains an important theme. As Alice's lifestyle has changed with age—she no longer works at the temple—and as she has entered a new environment—the retirement residence—service has taken on a different meaning. In the retirement residence, Alice categorizes other people by their service-orientation. She divides the individuals with whom she resides into two groups: those whose lives are empty and meaningless, and those who serve others and have contributed something to this world. She places most of the 300 people who share her surroundings in the first category and says of them: "They run around, trying to keep busy, filling their time with activities. What are they all rushing for? It's because they have nothing else." She places herself and her few friends in the second category, for she can feel compatible only with people who also hold this value and can present evidence of it in their life's work.

For example, she describes her two closest friends there in the following terms: One had worked hard at her profession as a college teacher in addition to having had full financial responsibility for a number of sick relatives. The other has had a strong religious orientation throughout life, and Alice says of her: "She is disciplined in her point of view. And she is consistent in her daily effort to reach spiritual things and to work, work, work, in trying to gain an inner insight that she longs for." Clearly, friends now are those who have held her determined, no-nonsense attitude toward life and who currently share her disdain for the "mad-house social life" that she feels most other people in this setting maintain. For Alice, people are judged by the values they share with her—especially work and social usefulness.

Clark's (1967; 1972; [Clark and Anderson] 1967) finding—that methods of realizing certain values in old age greatly influence emotional well-being and mental health—is highly relevant here. These case studies show how values that have been held for a lifetime are accommodated amid changes that accompany aging. The themes that emerge from these life stories illustrate the individuals' ability to reformulate lifelong values so that they (1) take on new meaning in old age, (2) promote a sense of continuity of self, and (3) contribute to an integrated and salient account of the life course.

For Mary, the observer-of-life theme emerges to supplement the wasteful-productive dichotomy theme when she talks about the present. The former serves as explanation of the value of productiveness in light of her current acceptance of her life course. Harold, when describing his retirement, brings new meaning to success and salesmanship by expanding their definitions to incorporate the value of social usefulness. For Alice, the themes of service and discipline are connected, first, to her long search for spiritual understanding. In discussing her current life however, these themes serve as a framework for understanding the people around her in the retirement residence. By accommodating existing themes to her present concerns, the values of work and social usefulness remain appropriate and relevant.

Five

The Ageless Self

The old are unsure of a future, their past has grown stale
so they are dependent on the sentience of the moment. It
behoves us to be sentient. Or—the old live by recalling
the past, and are fascinated by the query of what future is
possible. Their present is empty. Or—there is nothing
of interest to be said about the old, except that they are
absorbed by age. Each could be true. One takes one's
choice.

FLORIDA SCOTT-MAXWELL, AGE 82, *The Measure of
My Days*

The construction of a coherent, unified sense of self is an
ongoing process. We have seen how old people express
an identity through themes which are rooted in personal experience, particular structural factors, and a constellation of
value orientations. Themes integrate these three sources of
meaning as they structure the account of a life, express what
is salient to the individual, and define a continuous and creative self.

The sources of meaning which themes integrate are continually reinterpreted in light of new circumstances. A per-

son selects events from his or her past to structure and restructure his or her identity. Thus, themes continue to evolve from and give form to personal experience—making identity a cumulative process. At whatever point in time individuals construct their life stories, they pick and choose from a storehouse of memories and reflections. Reconstruction of the past and interpretation of one's self change as one grows older, as one has more experiences from which to choose and greater distance from which to evaluate past events. This is one reason themes "fit" together so well in a life story. Interpretations which have no explanatory or symbolic value at the time the story is told are weeded out and discarded. Continuous restructuring allows individuals to maintain a feeling of unity about themselves and a sense of connection with the parts of their pasts they consider relevant to who they are at present.

Personal identity as a phenomenon can be studied only in the present; the researcher cannot know about those themes which have been altered or abandoned, because the integration of experience takes place only through presently existing frameworks of understanding. The analyst cannot separate the past from the present in an oral life story; one can know the meaning of the past only through a person's current interpretation of it.[1] Because of this, the informant's identity (or major aspects of it) is shaped anew in the process of telling the story of his or her life.

Identity viewed as both cumulative process and current phenomenon may provide us with a way of understanding adult development over time and in a social context. Most theories of adult development implicitly assume that the individual life course follows a curve or trajectory—rising, arriving at a height of something (i.e., occupational success, social status, standard of living, positive self-image, etc.), and then falling back.[2] The concept of self often has been viewed from this paradigm with the aging individual seen as struggling to maintain a positive self-image—or succumbing to mental disorder or discontentment—in the face of declining health, social status, economic clout, power, and mobility. *The focus on themes in the lives of the elderly allows us to conceive of aging as continual creation of the self through the ongoing interpretation of past experience, structural factors, values, and current context.*

Identity is created and recreated over time as a person progresses through the life span. The structure and meaning of one's identity is established as experience is layered on experience and is simultaneously reflected upon, evaluated, adjusted to, and incorporated. But rather than being constructed to follow the rise and fall of an external trajectory through time, identity is built around themes, without regard to time, as past experiences are symbolically connected with one another to have meaning for a particular individual.

The elderly individuals I interviewed do not define themselves as being old. Study group members *know* they are old. They do not deny the fact. They are aware of the limits, physical and intellectual, imposed by old age, and they live within them. Moreover, they possess an awareness that their lives are without possibility: they unequivocally feel their lack of future. Nevertheless, they think of and describe themselves in terms of the themes they express as they reflect on their lives, rather than in terms of age. None of them has, at a certain juncture, created a new constellation of themes to coincide with the developmental stage of life called old age. The themes which appear to have evolved throughout the lives of these people are the themes through which they understand themselves and discuss their circumstances at present. Their conversations about their respective aging processes and the situations they must face as they grow older are framed in the thematic material they present.

Continuity of themes is, thus, a key element in the ageless identity of this particular elderly population and, I suspect, in the elderly in general. What can we say about the meaning of continuity in the individual life? Anthropologist Barbara Myerhoff notes that continuity in a life does not arise spontaneously, that it must be achieved. The individual *actively seeks* continuity as he or she goes through ordinary daily existence and interprets the circumstances with which he or she deals.[3] Millie, Ben, and Stella demonstrate the active search for continuity as they apply, adapt, and reformulate existing themes to new contexts so that a familiar and unified sense of self emerges in old age.[4]

Millie

Millie speaks of starting a "new life" when she moved into the Home, and she sees herself "improving" and "learning" all the time. She perceives her own aging as a process of renewal that began when she arrived at the institution. I asked her to look in the mirror and describe her image. She said: "I go by what people tell me. They say I look 100 percent better than I did. I have changed considerably from what I looked like when I first came here, and I see a more pleasant expression in my face, and I'm more inspired about my routine. . . ." Here, Millie's reference point for her self-description is other people's remarks about her improved morale and appearance since entering the institution.

In another interview, I asked Millie to describe herself. She replied: "I love people. I love the way they feel about me here, the attention." We know that she finds meaning in her relationships with people and that she thinks of herself only in terms of affective ties. Her current self-image is in keeping with this theme that is woven through her life story. As she views others in terms of their ties to her, so she sees herself as a product of social interaction. Continuous improvement and loving others are her specific self-descriptions at age 80. "Being old"—a state unrelated to other people—does not enter into her conceptual framework at all.

Millie's explanation of why she came to the Home, too, derives from her need for affiliation.

> Before I came here I was so lonely, I was afraid of going out of my mind. I'm not the type to sit around and watch TV and read magazines. That's why I came here. I like to mingle, to be around people, to have a room-mate, to have company. It's what my disposition needs.

Her family and physician probably would find the cause of her institutionalization elsewhere, most likely in the fact that she had a mild stroke and can no longer provide for all her physical needs.

Millie refers to her physical condition only when she feels she is being mistreated by others. In these instances, she uses her infirmities to manipulate interaction. Her body image is a device she employs to satisfy her needs and maintain other themes. For example, one morning she was quite distressed and complained to me that a nurse had offended her. She said: "I can't take it—in my condition. I'm a patient here. I don't have the strength to take that abuse." When someone does not treat her as she would like, she perceives herself as weak and ill, and then uses that identity as the reason she should not be abused. I never heard Millie refer to herself as a "patient" before or after this incident. This self-perception is clearly a survival tactic, and it is only called into play when needed to gain respect or take control of a situation.

As Millie describes her move to the nursing home, she speaks of taking control of her life for the first time. She claims to have changed her attitude and behavior in order to get what she wanted from her new environment. We have seen how she has been able to reorganize the institutional routine, structure her friendships, and invest casual encounters with affect through the creation of the theme self-determination. By establishing this new theme, Millie is able to maintain a viable self-image as she creates situations in which she acquires moral worth and social status.[5]

Another component in the formation of Millie's identity is her perception of her present relationship with her children. She says that she is happy living in the Home mainly because it pleases her children that she is there; she takes her cue for her own emotional state from them. For instance, she once stated to me: "When I tell my children of my accomplishments in classes, they say, 'Wonderful, Mother. I'm so glad to hear it.' . . . I'm so happy that they are thrilled because I'm here." She discusses her activities with them regularly by telephone and during their visits, and their reinforcement of her behavior seems to be crucial to the maintenance of her self-esteem and emotional well-being. She looks to her children for both feedback and encouragement for continuing with her specific pursuits in the Home and justification for living there at all. On several occasions, when she was depressed or angered by some incident in the Home, she broke down crying, and said: "If I didn't have my children to pull me through, I don't know what I'd do. They're everything to me." They provide her with a means of keeping up her morale and finding contentment in her present situation through an unspoken contract between them which reads: If my children are happy that I'm in the Home, then I must be happy about it too.

Yet, honoring the contract is not easy, for according to Millie, the relationship is far from satisfactory. Two children live in the same city as she does; they do not, according to her, visit enough. The other two live in another part of the country; apparently they do not communicate often enough by letter or telephone. Millie gets quite distraught if more than a week goes by without a visit and worries about her children's health, jobs, marriages, and children. Her peace of mind is forever being threatened by the perceived lack of attentiveness from them, and though she is surrounded by others who are sociable, she is lonely without constant communication from her children.

We recall that family members are devoted, attentive, and always available in Millie's thematic scheme; the worth of all relationships is measured by these qualities. In reality, the children do not always manifest all these traits. Though upset that her children do not meet her standards, Millie does not alter the theme to conform to their actual behavior or discard the theme outright. For it is the *theme*, not the children, which keeps Millie's identity intact. Through it, she is able to view her children as her primary and constant source of affection. This is her reason for living.

The theme also provides continuity. In order for Millie to continue perceiving herself as a loving and lovable person, her love for her children cannot falter, for they are the only stable outlet for her own love. Friends and acquaintances in the Home die or move away to hospitals. Staff members and volunteers come and go. But the relationship with children is permanent, whether or not they are visible. She can show her love for them in two ways—by honoring the unspoken contract, and by conceiving of her children in the ideal thematic framework she has constructed rather than focusing on their actual shortcomings.

Ben

I asked Ben if he feels as though he is 74. He said: "No, I don't. I feel the same as I did when I was much younger. . . . And as a matter of fact, I have a strong desire since my wife died to relive my coed days." When he looks back on his life, the years he spent in college stand out as the closest he was able to come to his "carefree," "romantic" self. His arrival in the college town in his early 20s symbolizes both his break away from the small town where he was raised and forced into a religious mold that he did not fit, and his first exposure to "big city" life and freedom. He recalls those days: "What a thrill it was to be there, and see four street car tracks, and all the excitement. I got a little Chevy coupe, and I started to date girls. And I enjoyed life as a single person."

Ben yearns to become what he remembers about that self now. When I asked what he was going to do about it, he replied: "I'm not doing anything about it, because you have to be your age, you know. . . . I could easily get going with a younger person. But I realize that would be unfair to the younger person and make a fool out of myself." The dichotomy-of-self theme which informs Ben's interpretation of his past also informs his perception of being old, and the discrepancy between the two selves creates a sense of frustration and futility.

On the one hand, Ben does not identify with his chronological age. He is healthy and has no physical ailments. He feels like a college student and he wants to act that way. On the other hand, he knows that to be 74 and to act 21 is socially inappropriate. With such a strong sense of propriety, he cannot ignore a lifetime of moral values and transcend the cultural assumptions of age-graded behavior. His worry about what other people and his "sober," "responsible" side would think prohibits him from becoming involved with a young woman.

The maintenance into old age of the theme dichotomy of self is evident also in Ben's comments about sex. "When I hear these jokes and stories about sex at 70, it almost revolts me. But then I realize *I'm* 74. I still have sex on my mind." He accepts the cultural stereotype that sex and old age are incompatible and indeed repulsive. But he also knows that the stereotype does not fit his own identity. The conflict of *feeling* one age and *being* another age is unresolved.

I asked Ben if he had any expectations while he was growing up of what being old would be like. He answered: "Ever since I was a youngster, I have thought of old people as infirm and sick. It was not a cheerful picture. Debilitation, fear of poverty, dependency. It wasn't a nice thing to look forward to." His fears of catastrophic illness and destitution, formed by his image of his father and his early family life, have largely shaped his conception of the aging process.

Ben's picture of aging is not completely negative, however. We recall that the theme religion is the framework for Ben's past and sets priorities for his future. Religion was a limitation for Ben through his early and middle years; it provided an ideal which he could not achieve and a guide from which he deviated. It stifled the development of his "carefree" self. He could never change his image of religion to fit his behavior. Now, late in life, religion is Ben's framework for imagining what the future will be like, and as such, it is the only positive component in his conception of aging. I asked him what he was going to do for the next 20 years. He replied:

> The older I get, and the less I'm able to do for people
> and the less use I'll be to them, I'll be narrowed down
> to the time when I will be alone and helpless except for
> whatever visitors choose to come, which I know won't
> be very many. So, if I didn't have that final resource, life
> would look very bleak to me. . . . I don't see how people
> can get along, why they aren't driven to great sadness
> by the fact that people are going to desert them. . . . I
> would call on my religious aids, on the parish priest,
> and I would expect him to reinforce my hopes about
> the next life.

Religion injects the only optimism into his view of aging and dying, because it provides him with an explanation of both the purpose of life on earth and life after death.

Ben's assumptions about what aging and dying will be like

reflect aspects of his disengagement theme as well. First, he supposes that he will become infirm and therefore will not be able "to do" for others: he fears he will end his life without fulfilling his need to be generous. Second, he expects to remain socially isolated until his death. And now in the context of the subject of aging, Ben explains his isolation as an outcome of his inability to help others. Third, he views "desertion" as a fact of aging. We know that Ben has no meaningful social relationships to give him a connection to the world of people. His feelings of ultimate abandonment stem from his lifelong experience of lack of permanence and supreme value in human relationships. Disengagement, the theme that emerges as Ben expresses his past and present style in the world, also defines his style, his sense of "expressive identifiability" (Goffman 1974) in the future, in his old age. The theme disengagement continues to have meaning for Ben, and though ultimately pessimistic, it provides an explanation of old age and a connection with his sense of himself at other times in his life.

Stella

I asked Stella how she felt about growing older. She replied:

> Age doesn't mean anything to me. I don't ever feel like I'm getting any older. I usually feel like I'm going to live forever. If I don't go around falling and having accidents, I might. . . . I never feel old until something happens. When I had my automobile accident, it took me a long time to get over it. That to me is old—when you begin to feel weak and shaking, and you can't do what you had been doing. I didn't think I was ever going to be well again, and I was going to be that way the rest of my life. [When] you gradually get well and get back to

work and you feel like yourself again—[you think]
you're never going to be old.

Stella does not think of herself as old except when she
cannot be active, when the expression of her achievement-
orientation theme is blocked. Old to her means the limitation of activity and productivity. She views herself as ageless;
only clumsiness on her part—"falling and having accidents"—can make her succumb to growing old.

Stella's ageless self is derived both from the themes she expresses as she describes her past and from her interpretation
of her present environment. We recall that the people in her
social world are at least a generation younger than she. Over
a period of several months, I observed her interactions with
the young people who work in the studio and found that they
do not act toward her as if she were old; they do not assume
her activity should be restricted or that she should be treated
in a certain way because she is 82. Rather, they perceive her
energy level and physical and mental capacities to be equal
to theirs, and in fact, they are. Their behavior toward her reinforces her own view of self as ageless. She once said to me:
"Somebody made the remark to me, 'You don't even talk like
you're old; you talk like you're the same age as whoever
you're talking to.' I said, 'That's the way I am.' I feel like I'm
the same age they are when I'm talking to them."

Stella expresses her agelessness (and implied sense of im-
mortality) in the promise to make better and better art all
the time—way into the future. Productivity and excellence,
regardless of the endeavor, are valued by the entire study
group as we have seen, but Stella places more emphasis on
these qualities at this stage of life than do any other informants. When I asked Stella what plans she has for the future,
she replied with conviction, "I am going to make a master-
piece!" And when I inquired at the beginning of a new year
what resolutions she had made, she answered, "I want to

turn out 365 pieces of sculpture this year, one every day, and I'm already behind." Stella's assertions are in marked contrast to the comments of other informants, many of whom stated to me: "I can't make any plans for the future now. I just live from day to day; that's the best I can do." Stella is trying to create something of lasting importance to the art world through tireless, creative effort.

The desire for continuity beyond her own life span extends to Stella's studio. She has poured herself into it and expects it will close when she dies. This is a major concern for her, and she spoke about it many times in our conversations. The studio is synonymous with life; she does not wish to see that life end. "My house and studio here—anybody I'd leave it to would sell it, just as soon as I die. But I don't want it to be that way. I don't want this place to be sold. I would rather I could make a permanent workshop out of it somehow." She discusses possible alternatives for keeping the studio a viable place after her death. Her wish for a permanent studio is not shared by others and she knows this. She talks about this problem in terms of the selflessness theme. "These kids, they only think of themselves. I suppose they think the studio will continue forever. They don't plan ahead at all." Just as she feels the daily upkeep of the studio rests ultimately on her, so she perceives its existence after her death as her sole responsibility.

Stella's preoccupation with a permanent studio underscores her selfless approach to life and the desire for continuity beyond her own life span; she envisions giving to others and creating art after she is gone. Preservation of the studio would immortalize these aspects of her identity. Moreover, Stella needs her personal efforts to be carried on by others just as she carried on her mother's productivity and her daughter's art. Since she has no living descendants to establish her biological continuity with the future, she needs "these kids" to act as her family, preserving what is important to her. In this way, they would symbolize a familial link with succeeding generations. Finally, the studio is her most important creation. Stella wants it, as a tangible object, to have an impact on the future as a work of art can. As the visible and symbolic edifice of her creative process, it could immortalize her identity as an artist. More than the other people I interviewed, Stella looks beyond her own life span as she seeks continuity.[6]

All research participants made it clear to me that *aging* per se is not a substantive issue in their own lives. They do not, now that they are over 70, conceive of themselves in a context of *aging* and act accordingly. Rather, they deal with specific problems, changes, and disabilities as they arise, just as they have been doing throughout their lives, and they interpret these changes and problems in the light of already established themes. It appears that the concept of aging is too abstract, too impersonal to be an integral part of identity. This is not to say that my informants ignore or deny their own aging and the discomforts and limitations which arise in that process. Nor does it mean that the changes experienced in old age have no psychological effects. But while dealing with the physical and mental manifestations of old age, old people also maintain an ageless sense of self that transcends change by providing continuity and meaning.

What is the meaning of this sense of timelessness for the field of gerontology? The concept of adaptation has traditionally channeled most research in social gerontology and has attributed certain characteristics to the nature of the aging process. The gerontologists George Maddox and James Wiley (1976:15) state, "The relationship between aging and successful adaptation (variously morale or life satisfaction or mental health) is perhaps the oldest, most persistently investigated issue in the social scientific study of aging." The meaning attributed to adaptation which has, by and large,

shaped nearly 40 years of research is contentment. Simić
(1978: 16) has noted that research aimed at discovering and
evaluating levels of contentment, problematic in itself, reflects an American ethnocentrism which supposes that
"happiness" is what one strives for in old age. A basic prem-
ise of this view is that any state of being other than "happiness" is detrimental to the individual and is to be avoided
if at all possible. Besides the empirical and methodological
problems this view entails, the definition itself traps the in-
vestigator into looking at questions that deal with the presence, absence, and quantity of contentment in later life, a
narrow scope for aging research.

In research formulated to define or measure adaptation, individual members of the population being studied are largely
interchangeable; details of the individual life are of no consequence. However, if one investigates the individual life
course and how meaning is obtained from it, the concept of
adaptation can be broadened. Recent work in the field of life-
span development has contributed to a broader conceptual-
ization of adaptation through studies of the subjective meaning of change and continuity in the individual life course (for
example: Cohler 1982; Kotre 1984; Ryff 1984). These works
and others lend support to the idea that *successful adaptation takes place when individuals symbolically connect
meaningful past experiences with current circumstances.*
Adaptation in late life must be conceived as more than striving for contentment; it is also the process by which a person
creates meaning, organizes the past, explains events, and
communicates with others. Adaptation viewed in these
terms allows research in gerontology to address the operat-
ing frameworks of the elderly themselves. The thematic
analysis of life-story material reveals the phenomenological
understanding of self as ageless to show us that "morale" and
"life satisfaction" are not necessarily key factors in the determination of behavior. Instead, construction and inter-

pretation of experience as one grows older are found to be critical elements that give form and meaning to one's actions.

What does the concept of the ageless self tell us about the popular notion of aging as nothing but losses—sensory, functional, economic, social? In recent years, researchers have shown that the aging process is more than deprivation and forfeiture to which one must succumb and, it is hoped, adjust.[7] For old people continue to participate in society, and more than this, old people continue to *interpret* their participation in the social world. By looking at themes that emerge from their own stories, we can see how the old not only cope with the losses, but how they create new meaning as they reformulate and build viable selves. Thus, creating identity is a lifelong process.

Six

Coming to Terms

Old paint on canvas, as it ages, sometimes becomes
transparent. When that happens it is possible, in some
pictures, to see the original lines: a tree will show
through a woman's dress, a child makes way for a dog, a
large boat is no longer on an open sea. That is called
pentimento because the painter "repented," changed his
mind. Perhaps it would be as well to say that the old
conception, replaced by a later choice, is a way of seeing
and then seeing again. . . . The paint has aged now and
I wanted to see what was there for me once, what is
there for me now.

LILLIAN HELLMAN, *Pentimento*

The life stories created by the elderly people who participated in this study dispel some of the negative stereotypes of aging in American society. During the collection and
analysis of their accounts, I discovered that "being old" is
not central to the self-perceptions of these people over 70
and that these people have not created an "aged role" for
themselves. After 70, there is less "becoming"—fitting into
prescribed roles, taking on socially required identities, ac-

quiring positions of social status—than at any other time in the life cycle. True, socialization continues as elderly individuals take on such new roles as widow or widower and grandparent for example, as they move and adjust to retirement residences or nursing homes, and as they cope with a variety of losses. The point is that old people are not caught up in socialization *to* old age,[1] nor are their self-concepts based upon socialization to any particular role that might be acquired *in* old age.

Practicing gerontologists deplore the fact that there is no positive, valued role for the aged in the United States. The gerontological literature assumes that meaning in old age, or "successful adaptation" to old age, can be found only in the continuation of roles acquired at an earlier life stage, or the creation of new roles in late life. Anthropologists, seeking to understand the nature of elderly social status through cross-cultural comparisons, have described the variety of roles (many of honor, dignity, and high status) awarded to elderly members of small-scale, nonindustrial societies and explained that the absence of roles for the aged in American society is due to demographic, historical, and ideational factors.

Interactionist theory has tended to emphasize the construction of self through reality created and roles represented in current interactions—the self defined through interpretation of a moment in time rather than through interpretation of the meaning of accumulated time. Interactionists have stressed socialization and situational adjustment as key processes of social life and adult development. Consequently, change—rather than continuity, coherence, or integration—is viewed as the essential outcome.

These case studies present a different view: the self employing the past as a resource for creating meaning in present encounters. Thus the retention of past roles, the acquisition of new roles, and the act of playing out roles are not necessarily cornerstones of identity in old age. Yet, individuals do retain and create a sense of self to the end of their lives. For, as these cases have shown, though role creation and maintenance are important, the self is conceived in broader terms than social role. Identity formulation includes more than the sum of statuses acquired over the life span, more than descriptions of becoming, and then being, a "mother," "worker," "grandparent," "widow," etc. Individuals draw from a larger scheme to create a continuous self in old age. We have seen that they draw from structural factors that limit or broaden their choices throughout life and from shared values to formulate an identity. In addition, people draw from cultural expectations and assumptions about "becoming" and "being" through the life span. And then, they compare and integrate memories of self with their present condition and knowledge of self. In looking back, individuals create a self by coming to terms with cultural expectations of how one's life should have been—the possibilities that were, and now are, available. As the themes of these informants indicate, social roles taken, missed, or rejected are only one dimension of this formulation.

Shared assumptions and expectations about how an individual life should be lived are part of every society; they include: stages and timing of biological and social development, patterns of socialization, work and leisure, requirements of family life and household, and constraints and opportunities of gender, ethnic group membership, and socioeconomic position. These shared assumptions—also called pathways[2] or life plans[3]—are one's cultural heritage, the normative ideas about the shape and meaning of the individual life course. They provide context for personal reflection and identity formulation throughout the life span. Though American elderly enact no explicit, positive roles through which they can define themselves, every old American, as a cultural being, has ideas about the course his or her own life has taken *in relation* to ideal pathways. And, every old person interprets this relationship—between his or her own development and cultural ideals—to formulate a sense of self for the present and to negotiate a meaningful future, however short.

The broad pathway characteristic of my informants' age cohort and their Caucasian, Judeo-Christian background set the stage for individual notions about the kind of person one should strive to be and how to become that kind of person. Perfectability of human existence through education, work, good deeds, and freedom of choice was perhaps the cornerstone of this pathway, a cluster of ideas shaping these individuals' notions of "becoming" in American society. An individual's potential for following this pathway was determined by both opportunities of mobility, financial gain, interpersonal relationships, and the personality traits of perseverance ("stick-to-itiveness"), strong moral fiber ("follow the Golden Rule"), and ambition. Christopher Lasch (1979) has characterized the period during which my informants grew up, established their identities, and lived most of their lives as one of "competitive individualism." The slogans repeated by many informants as they formulate their philosophies of life attest to this assumption of how a life should be lived. "Give a little; take a little"; "Make the most of what you've got"; "Do the best you can"; and "Pull yourself up by your own bootstraps." We have seen how the informants account for these overarching parameters of American existence as they create themes to formulate their senses of self now.

Pathways are, of course, made more elaborate and explicit by one's specific cultural heritage and one's gender. We recall that in her youth Millie's immigrant pathway prescribed cultural assimilation—"joining the melting pot" and "becoming thoroughly modern and Americanized." The life expectations she shared at that time with female contemporaries

were to marry, raise at least several children, and, work along-
side one's husband to achieve financial stability, material
comfort, constancy of family life, and perpetual security.
Ben's pathway has been one of maintenance through spiritual sustenance: life has been an attempt to hold onto one's
physical and economic status in the face of great odds. Life
stage transitions have been prescribed by fear of loss and the
quest for inner strength with which to cope with loss by
retrenchment in traditional, religious values. In contrast,
Stella's pathway has embodied a different American experience—that of pioneer. Her life expectations have included
many symbols of the frontier: freedom to roam and explore,
a heightened sense of adventure and independence, and the
promise of a tomorrow full of possibility. Turning to the case
material of Millie, Ben, and Stella once more, we see how
they interpret the relationship between cultural pathway and
self at the end of their lives.

   Unlike the people Barbara Myerhoff describes in *Number
Our Days* (1979), Millie is not self-consciously Jewish. She
is not a product of an orthodox, religious tradition, nor is she
steeped in "Yiddishkeit," the traditional, Eastern European,
shtetl folk culture of the Jews.[4] I infer from Millie's account
that her parents broke away from their religious tradition
when they immigrated to America. Millie says she had no
formal religious training as a child and, indeed, was not exposed to Jewish rituals and ceremonies while she lived at
home. Millie's assimilation into secular America was started
by her mother. Millie recalls: "She only spoke German and
English at home. She was as Americanized and modern as
she could be. I had no religious upbringing whatever. . . ."
Millie states that her first meaningful contact with religion
came when she met the family of her first husband. "The
first Yiddish I ever heard was when I got acquainted with my
in-laws. They were Jewish to the core. But my [first] husband

was not religious either." Nevertheless, Millie's assimilation into her ethnically diverse childhood neighborhood was not complete. Although she mentions playing with children from other ethnic backgrounds, her four closest childhood friends, who were the best friends she ever had and whom she describes in some detail, were from German-Jewish immigrant families as she was. The fact that she remained intimate for many years with these childhood friends of similar ethnic background attests to her early identification as a Jew.

The melting pot ideal remained in Millie's life, but it was constantly challenged by Millie's affirmations of Jewish identity as she married, raised her children, observed their marriages, and came to depend on them and others for her care. Now, as she reflects on the path of her life and the lives of her grown children, she notes that she has had to accept much more cultural assimilation than she would have liked. She presents the diffused, ideal "Americanized" identity as a mirror in which her core Jewish self is always reflected.

I asked Millie if she gave her children a Jewish upbringing. She replied: "No, the only one that was brought up as a Jew was my oldest son. And he was bar mitzvahed. But the others had nothing, after their father died." Her Jewishness apparently did not play an active part during her childrearing years, and Millie has nothing to say about being a Jew as she discusses that aspect of her past.

In contrast, she has much to say about her children's marriages, all in the context of who is and is not Jewish. Millie has felt disappointed by the assimilation of the next generation. Her eldest son (who was bar mitzvahed) is described as nearly perfect and as the only child living up to Millie's theme of affective ties.

My oldest son, wait 'til you see him. And his wife—he is the only one that married a Jewish girl. I adore her; I love her. If you read the letters she writes to me, and her son is the lawyer you know. And, they are coming out here to live. They are going to build a home. They bought a lot here, and they are gradually getting rid of their other property, and will move here to be near me and their friends. They are very close to my family, very. And B. is not a step-sister; B. is one of them. They idolize her. E.'s marriage is a love-affair from A to Z. His wife is not beautiful, but she is interesting looking, and a wonderful, lovely person. She's ideal to me, like a daughter, and very anxious to come out here and live.

Millie's next child, a daughter, is described as follows:

S. was married in Brooklyn to a Jewish boy. Very young, she was a pretty thing and boy-conscious. They were political, and their politics didn't interest me. I wasn't enthused about it, but I never interfered. Something to do with socialism or something. But he died early.

Millie lived with this daughter for a time, after the daughter was widowed and Millie had divorced her second husband. Millie recalls that period as "a happy, satisfied time." Later, when Millie had remarried for the third time and moved away, she received a letter from this daughter.

She wrote me a letter and told me, inadvertently, that she was remarried, and she didn't tell me, but between the lines I could tell that it was a black man she married. My husband was very democratic. Anything anybody in the family did was OK with him. He never criticized or ridiculed her; he was very fond of her. . . . When I met [my daughter's husband], he took me for a day's outing, and he impressed me greatly. But at heart, I wasn't too thrilled. I even feel to this day that my daughter should have married someone like her, but I never made an issue of it, never told her one word to make her upset or that I felt she did the wrong thing.

Millie refers to the children from this marriage as "my black grandsons," and she is forever worrying about their problems as they go through adolescence and young adulthood.

In the context of describing her youngest daughter's accomplishments, Millie told me:

> B. talks Persian. She took it up specifically to be able to talk to her mother-in-law, who lives near them. They adore each other. [Her mother-in-law] is a Muslim to the core. With a veil and from the old school. And she calls me here on the phone and says, "Mama darling, I love you." And everytime she comes to see me, she brings me a gift. The first gift was a Persian runner. The second gift was an 18-carat gold chain with a thick gold piece—worth $75.

Millie sums up her sense of self in relation to her family:

> I feel I'm a Jew at heart, even though there was so little in my family. My family is everything: Persian, black, Protestant, Catholic. One sister has been a Christian Scientist for 30 years. And I had a Catholic sister-in-law who was better than a daughter to my mother. But we're all people, and we love each other, and there is no dissension, no dissension.

The individuals who inhabit Millie's employment history are described by their non-Jewish identities and as contrast-other. As Millie talks about her success in work, her ability to get jobs wherever she went, she stresses her adaptive capacity, her ability to get along with, conform to, and be liked by different ethnic groups wherever she has gone.

> My boss at one place never hired Jews. I was the only Jewish employee. They always considered me a desirable person. . . . I love people. And I worked with Gentiles, blacks, and Chinese. The place I worked 12 years,

the boss was a Chinaman. And I loved meeting the
black people. I made friends with them. They always
credited me with my ability. . . .

Looking back, Millie feels she successfully blended into the
American mainstream—in her case an amalgam of other
ethnic groups.

Most recently, just before moving to the nursing home,
Millie lived for three years in a retirement residence she
describes as "99 percent black." She says: "They gave me a
gorgeous room there, and I made a lot of friends. Although
the black people are very clannish, they made friends with
me. I formed a knitting school, and they were very pleased
with me."

Then Millie had a stroke. While she was hospitalized, her
children told her she would be going to the nursing home
where she now resides, a facility run by and for the local Jewish community. Millie says that her children told her it was
not a "convalescent hospital," and not a "nursing home" but,
rather, a "Jewish home." They told her, "Mother, you won't
be alone. You will be happy there." Millie recalls:

I was scared to death. I wanted to go back to the retirement residence, even though I knew it wasn't the best
place for me. I couldn't mess up my kids' lives by moving in with them. I had been here once to see a friend
of mine a long time ago, but I had forgotten about this
place. I forgot it existed. But I had been around Jewish
people. And I am a Jew at heart.

Ironically, Millie's assimilated children expressed their
own cultural heritage by placing her in this facility. Because
the children chose a Jewish nursing home, Millie tells herself that they are not rejecting her. Millie accents their decision as natural and inevitable and, in fact, is pleased that the
children activated their Jewishness. Their decision under-

scores their return to the family heritage, apparently after many years of distance from it. Thus, Millie is "thankful" that she is in this home, and by being there, she concurs with her children and retains a "close and loving" relationship with them.

I asked Millie how she felt about living in a Jewish environment after all these years. She told me:

> I'm so glad I'm here. There's something about Gentiles.
> I've had to adapt, to become worldly, out of necessity.
> I'll never forget my childhood friends, Florence,
> Minnie, and Gussie. We were like that (places four fingers together). So clannish, always together. And after
> we were married, we wrote letters back and forth, and
> an X in the upper right corner meant you were
> pregnant.

> But I've had to associate with more people now than
> when I was young, and different types of people, and
> express myself differently, I think.

> I really wonder myself how I came to be so attached to
> people here. Is it just because I'm living here, is it because of my nature, or is it because I'm Jewish?

I believe the answer lies in all three explanations. Millie's theme of affective ties is her way of expressing her "nature," her innermost self. She expresses this theme as she interprets relationships with her co-residents to keep from falling apart in the institutional setting. The fact that the other residents are Jewish makes the formulation process easier. Throughout life she has had no alternative but to "join the melting pot," that is, to seek acceptance from ethnically different co-workers and co-residents in order to survive, and, as important, to create the personal attachments she needs. Finally, at the end of her life, assimilation is no longer a requirement for her emotional well-being.

Millie expected to belong to the American mainstream and has lived her entire life accordingly. She followed this pathway both out of necessity and in order to pursue a cultural ideal. Though Millie traveled this pathway and evaluated herself by it, she experiences herself now as having always been separate from it.

Constancy of family life and security derived from constancy have been the other primary components of Millie's life plan. Her deviation from this ideal was due to the unfortunate and unexpected realities of her existence: the death of her first husband, poor relationship with her second husband, and lack of love for her third husband. These realities caused profound upheavals and long-lasting discontinuity in her family life which she could not rectify, though she tried. Millie married three men, but she refers only to the first as "my husband," adding, "although I did live with these other two men." She regards the first husband as the man who should have been her mate for the rest of her days. The second and third men were merely substitutes. Their role was to enable Millie to keep to her life plan, and each marriage was an attempt to restore what had been lost in the one before.

But with the termination of each marriage, Millie moved further away from her expectations, and she turned to family members in other parts of the United States for financial and emotional support. She moved around the country to stabilize the family, but the moves only gave her a greater sense of dislocation and emphasized her distance from the ideal pattern she sought.

Millie recalls that "the home broke up" after her first husband died. She married the second man to reestablish a home for herself and her children, but she describes the turn of events as follows:

> First, he wanted to accept my children, and we made a household together. And then he found fault with my children and threw them out. He threw them out.

They went to live by themselves and insisted I stay with him. These children brought themselves up without me, without a father, without a mother, had to be on their own. All on their own—what can I tell you?

That marriage ended unhappily, and the widening gap between the ideal pathway and Millie's actual course devastated her. She explains her divorce: "I was so ashamed—divorce at that time—I felt like a woman scorned. And I was ashamed to look at anybody, and when anybody talked to me, I felt on edge."

After the divorce, Millie took her new baby and moved to a different state to live with her daughter. She recalls that when her ex-husband did not send her money, she had nothing. Nevertheless, she speaks of that time in her daughter's household as "satisfying." The daughter subsequently moved to California, "leaving" Millie in the East, stranded, without a home once again. So Millie moved to the South to live with a brother and sister-in-law. "They wanted to adopt my baby. I said, 'Listen, nobody can adopt my baby.' They adored that child." According to Millie, they talked her into marrying again, for "security" and, more symbolically, for a last grasp at what was supposed to be. But the third husband was sick, and Millie and he moved to a drier climate for his health, leaving the child behind with her brother until they could find a place to live. Though they came back for the baby, they never settled down, and the husband remained sickly. After more years of moving from apartment to apartment, they finally relocated to California to be with Millie's grown daughter. Millie's youngest child was now 15. The possibility of creating and sustaining a rich and stable family life was gone.

As Millie examines her life from the vantage point of 80 years, she articulates the many discrepancies between her expectations on the one hand and the development of her unique career on the other. She cannot narrow the gap created by a lifetime of circumstance and choice; she cannot re-live the past. But in the institution, she assesses the path she has traveled, the person she has become, to recreate what is important now in light of the existing discrepancies. The themes that emerge from her life story account for the gap between the actual and the ideal.

Millie's normative pathway has been an ideal she could only attempt to achieve throughout her life. Ben, on the other hand, has remained close to expected standards, though he has always wanted to break away from them.

Ben grew up in an Irish Catholic environment in which earthly life was characterized as precarious; both security and meaning were to be sought in service to God. Ben was expected to serve God by becoming a priest. That pathway required "devotion." Ben wanted "an education" instead, and he left that path to attend college. The ideal life plan was narrowly constructed by Ben's family—the priesthood or nothing. In leaving the Catholic order, Ben jumped into a cultural abyss.

> I worried for years. At that time, life was a lot more serious. When people would join the priesthood, and changed their minds midstream, it was labeled "losing your vocation." It was not called changing your mind or your plans. God had called you to this specialized task, and you had not been generous enough to respond.
> They used to point to that with pride. They used to say, "It takes seven candidates to make a member." But they should have said, "Six people out of seven give it up." Now, they are much more liberal, much more in-telligent about people leaving. But at the time I left, it was traumatic.

Though relieved by his choice, Ben was also painfully aware that he was no longer doing what he should. Ben re-jected the priesthood, but he did not abandon his religion or

deviate from its moral imperatives. Thus, his actual path
was as close to his family's ideal as he could manage. Ben's
life story at age 74 is an assessment of the path he followed.
Each step, each decision, produced conflict, for he could not
realize the ideal of devotion laid before him, nor could he become the exciting adventurer he imagined. His actual development did not fulfill either potential. As he looks back now,
he gauges his distance from both the cultural expectation
and the personal desire.

Most of his life course decisions contributed to his "sober," "steady," "responsible" self and kept him close to the
expectations of his cultural milieu. Of his marriage, he says:

> I guess if it hadn't been for religion, I would have
> walked out long before. When people realized how in-
> hibited my life was, they said, "How do you stand it?
> You're either a very virtuous guy, or there's something
> the matter with you." I had a friend next door. He had
> a lovely wife, but he was always looking around, dating
> younger girls, spending weekends with them. It was a
> sexual thing, and he was always advising me. I envied
> him. But when you're brought up to believe that the
> marriage vows mean what they say, in sickness and in
> health, why then you feel very guilty if you attempt to
> stray from it.

> A lot of people would have said that the relationship
> was an unhealthy one. It would have been healthier if I
> had left, healthier for both of us. I couldn't quite see
> how it would have been any better for her, and I would
> have felt terribly guilt-ridden.

I asked Ben why he stayed with his boring job. He replied:

> Security. I had an invalid wife, for whom I would al-
> ways need another $10,000 a year. . . . It was such an
> easy job; I was doing it in my sleep. And I wasn't adven-

turous enough to quit. And I don't know, what would I
have done if I did quit? If somebody had come along,
some aggressive person who said, "Look, we can make
a fortune in real estate. You can be my partner in this,"
or something, I would have jumped at it, see? But nobody came along, and I just stayed in my rut.

Ben's actual path did not measure up to his family's standard or his own romantic fantasy. Now, no longer faced with
marital or financial responsibility, Ben does not choose the
"carefree" path—he has not planned that trip he claims he
wants to "exotic" South America. Instead, he still accounts
for what he "should" do, such as visit dying patients in hospitals. But he cannot bring himself to do this; he told me,
"You see, all the worthwhile things in life are horribly dull."
Ben is caught between the narrow expectations and the desire to be free, yet bitterness and regret do not overwhelm his
story. His theme of religion—reinterpreted now—sustains
him, satisfies him, and bridges the gaps between the person
he is, the kind of person he should have been, and the identity he has wanted. He talks about the meaning of religion in
his life more than anything else. Though he refused to accept the role of priest, Ben's life is imbued with religious
faith. He explains:

> You either have the gift of faith, or you don't. There are
> many fine people who investigate the Catholic faith or
> other Christian faiths, and they just cannot say, "Yes, I
> do believe in this." They don't experience conversion.
> They keep trying to reason, but you can't reason your
> way into faith. It's a gift.

Religious faith has brought meaning to Ben's actual path. It
has provided emotional stability and has anchored his sense
of self as no acquired roles—priest, teacher, husband, bureaucrat—were ever able to do. Ben told me:

Fundamentally, I'm wrapped up in a sort of notion of a divine romance between creatures and Creator. You see, I never lost my religious background. Even while I was indifferent to it, I had that feeling that I'm the center of the universe. I'm participating in a divine romance. . . .

I recently read an astronomy book, and according to the author, the largest thing in the universe is the greatest red star. The smallest thing is the electron. And right in between, in the middle, was man. Man was in the center. Of course, I have a religious interpretation of all this. But I can really get enthusiastic about this—the fantastic miracles that surround us. I used to give talks about that subject to a club I belonged to.

I think God is so mysterious and so indescribable that we have to sort of give up. But that doesn't mean He doesn't love me, doesn't watch me very closely so that He literally knows when a hair falls from my head, just as He knows when a sparrow falls and all that sort of thing. And if that turns out to have been an illusion, then it was a nice dream. And it's sustained me in times when otherwise I would have been desolate. So, I don't see how I can lose.

Ben formulates a sense of future through his religious faith as well.

To me, death is not a tragedy at all. You know, this whole business, everyone wants to go to heaven, but nobody wants to die. That's foolish. Nobody wants to suffer a great deal, that's true. But we shouldn't be afraid of death if it's going to be a better life.

And it won't matter. I'm living one illusion and the atheist is living with another illusion. He could be wrong. And meanwhile, the two of us—my illusion is a much more gratifying illusion than his. He is living in a sterile, pointless world where he postpones explaining life.

So, the big drive in my life now is looking forward to the next life. I believe that someone is looking out for me.

Ben had abandoned a pathway and left a dream unfulfilled. But as he describes himself and integrates his own development with cultural ideals, he formulates a meaningful directive for the rest of his life.

Of these three informants, Stella has had perhaps the broadest pathway: an expectation of unlimited opportunity in an expanding world. The cultural environment of her childhood instilled the ideal of the self-made person and the fact that autonomy must be earned by diligent, productive labor. She grew up on the American frontier: her father moved west, homesteading, to be entirely independent from his wife's family. The "pioneer spirit," developed early on, has shaped her entire life. Within her family, Stella was never restricted by her sex, never constrained from personal choice-making because she was female. On the contrary, her parents encouraged their daughters to become whatever they wanted.

Stella recalls playing on the farm and ranch of her childhood as the happiest moments of her life. Though there were always many chores, it is remembered as the only carefree time of her life, a time for doing whatever she wanted. I asked her to describe her child self. She told me:

I was a tomboy. I always wanted to play with the boys. My friends were the boys. I was always getting into mischief. . . . When I was about six, my father gave me a calf. We lived on a cattle ranch then. He was my pet. And I tied a rope around his middle. And he'd run

around a lot, all over the farm, and I'd ride it, just like
you would a horse. And later, I got older, and my father
gave me a pony.

When Stella was older, her parents moved closer to a town
so the children could attend high school. Later she wanted to
move to a larger city by herself to pursue a college education,
and her parents encouraged her to go. Without formal education themselves, they wanted to help educate all their children. They could offer no financial assistance, but the pattern of their lives were models to Stella of self-determination
and accomplishment. From childhood, she was encouraged
to pursue her dreams, to become whatever she chose.

The father moved the family many times for economic
opportunity. He moved to better farmland during drought
years; he started a variety store where none existed. A free
spirit, he was not one to be tied down. The mother was an
opportunist and entrepreneur. She farmed, worked in the
store, and bartered her cooking skills for the children's music
lessons. According to Stella, she became many things, and
excelled at them all.

Shortly after Stella began her college education, World War
I began. She saw her sister and friends taking new jobs in industry and earning more money than they ever had before,
and she was inspired to do the same. She quit college, took a
business course, and got a clerical job which she held for
three years, until the war ended and the company closed
down.

Seeking to broaden her horizons, she drove out to Oregon
with some relatives. She expresses her pioneer self in her description of that journey west.

There were no motels. We camped along the way. We
had a very small car and had luggage piled everywhere.
There was barely room for me to sit. We saw animal
skulls and bones along the roadside—sometimes there

was no road at all. Whenever we did come to a town we got our gas in cans. . . . Sometimes we met other folks in old cars. Everyone was friendly. It was just like the covered wagon days.

As soon as they arrived in a large town, Stella left her relatives and struck out on her own. She immediately found herself an apartment and a job. In many ways the opposite of Ben, Stella has always forged ahead into the unknown; that was her life plan, her expectation of how life should be lived. She says however: "I always had to do things my own way. I learned by making mistakes. I don't learn by doing something right, hardly ever." Her biggest "mistake" was marrying the wrong man. Stella says her mother and her friends were against the marriage, saying he was not "the marrying kind." Stella paid no attention to them and, looking back, regrets her choice. He was unfaithful and they divorced shortly after her daughter was born.

During the years she was raising her child alone, Stella enjoyed being a housewife. She says she ironed, washed, cleaned house, and did what she was "supposed" to do. Having a family and maintaining a household were part of the pioneer-housewife pathway. Her mother had done it—productively, creatively, ceaselessly. Stella could not attain that identity because the marriage ended, there were no more children, and finally the daughter died. But then Stella began to study art, and in this endeavor, this career, she was able to become the kind of person she expected to be—self-made, talented, versatile, and a creative force for younger generations to emulate.

Undaunted by lack of experience, Stella says she stumbled along at first. In telling her story, she recalls many embarrassing moments because "I wouldn't listen, and I had to do things on my own. I never did exactly what someone else asked." For example, she told me:

My art teacher asked us to go to the exhibit at the museum. There was a picture done by one artist. He does dark pictures, always a sad look, and the museum was full of his pictures. I wondered, how on earth did this ever get into the museum? You want to look at something sad? Pictures should be beautiful. They should make you feel happy and good. That's what I thought anyway.

So, in class I said, "How in the world did those pictures get in the museum? I didn't think they'd allow pictures like that in the museum." The teacher said, "Why?" I said, "They're too depressing. They just make you feel miserable. I think pictures should be beautiful, make you feel happy."

Well, I overspoke. I have a history of that. Saying things before I thought them out. Before I knew what I was talking about. The teacher didn't say a word, he just stayed quiet for about a minute, you know, a *long* minute. And I looked around at everybody and I felt so embarrassed. So I went home. Nobody said anything to me after class. I went home and went to the library. I got books out on that artist. And I studied. . . . I got so that he was my favorite painter. Oh, I thought he was wonderful before I got through with him—knew him. That's the way I learned, by just spitting it out, by making mistakes.

Stella forged ahead, tirelessly, going to art classes in the evenings after work, seeking out new teachers, exploring different media, experimenting with techniques. She tried many things before finally establishing her identity as a sculptor and painter.

Over the past 40 years, Stella has never ceased expanding her horizons as an artist. For a time, she lived communally with other artists, so she could afford to have a studio as well. She bought several homes, converting them to studio/ workshops, moving when they restricted her artistic growth and became too small to teach the growing number of students who came to her for classes. At her current location, there is enough space for classes, and various independent artists rent workshop space for themselves as well.

She has continued to take art courses, meet artists, and seek out innovation in the arts throughout her career. A few months before our interviews began, she took a two-month trip to Romania to study folk arts. She traveled all over the country, meeting artists and visiting studios and museums. She had a translator accompany her. She returned newly inspired and motivated. Stella, at age 82, is actively traveling the pioneer pathway still.

Though Stella's urge to create and explore remains strong, her lack of family is a growing source of sadness and concern as she gets older. I asked Stella to describe the best thing about growing older. She replied:

> Is there something good? I think it would be fine if
> I had a big family around me. If I had my children and
> everything, and could be a grandmother. It would be
> swell to have everything like that. But I don't have any-
> one close to me now, and that's a little sad.

This is one aspect of Stella's life plan that remains unfulfilled. Now, Stella worries about her deteriorating eyesight and her future, because there will be no children to care for her when she can no longer be self-sufficient.

Perfectability of self is generally thought to be accomplished by traveling the cultural pathway. These individuals account for themselves, identify themselves, through norms and expectations of how a life should be lived. Millie craved the expected life plan, but never attained it. She is no longer becoming—the distance from her ideal is too great and the opportunities have passed. Nevertheless, she describes herself in the context of the ideal: she *is* that kind of person—committed to making and maintaining strong emotional bonds, especially with family, satisfied with those relationships, successful in both assimilation and in employment, secure in her environment—though she could not realize the normative path. Her themes bridge the gap between the possibilities of her youth and the actual turn of events, and they make it possible for her to integrate the ideal with the actual as she reflects on her life.

Ben rejected the explicit pathway set before him but has retained the underlying tenets of that pathway throughout his life, though every chance to deviate from these tenets was fraught with conflict. His lifelong dilemma has been to integrate the fact that he embraced the philosophy of the life plan with his desire to abandon it. His dichotomous self-image expresses his lifelong lack of resolution. But his renewed religious faith is his deepest meaning in late life.

Stella has realized her life plan—to fulfill the promise of the frontier. Unable to turn life's challenges into achievements as a pioneer housewife on a rural, western landscape, she became an artist. With that emerging identification, Stella turned the tragedy of her daughter's death into an opportunity for personal exploration and gratification. Though she continues to seek artistic accomplishments and is never fully satisfied, she has achieved many goals of her pioneer pathway—autonomy, self-determination, creativity, and productivity—in her own time and in her own way.

There are moments during the life course when people choose, or are persuaded by circumstance, to evaluate or become conscious of the direction of their lives. Attaining, rejecting, or missing critical stages or turning points—marriage, career, the birth of a child, the death of a spouse—are such moments. Telling the life story in old age is another such moment, an occasion for comparing the life lived with the prescribed directive. The life stories of these elderly

Americans illustrate their continued, vital involvement with cultural pathways at the end of their lives and their ability to seek and create new meaning as they interpret their pasts. Their stories, in fact, take shape in the process of coming to terms with their particular heritage, a process that will continue as long as they are sentient. In old age, people make new assessments of themselves as they create an integrated identity, account for the paths they have traveled, and formulate meaning for the rest of their lives.

The cultural pathways of Millie, Ben, and Stella are characteristically American. To assimilate, to live by a set of religious principles in a secular land, to conquer frontiers—these are uniquely American goals, American problems. And, these are profound cultural issues in the lives of my 60 elderly informants. These goals, with their inherent conflicts and tensions, shaped the direction of their lives. Now, they are both the framework for evaluating the past and the context for self-knowledge.

Assimilation is perhaps the most compelling cultural issue for all immigrants and their children. Millie's life story exemplifies this aspect of American existence. There can be no doubt that the value placed on assimilation has changed since the first years of this century. For other immigrants in this study, and for Millie's generation in general, the question was: How can I leave the old ways behind and *become an ideal American?* The question today's immigrant poses is different: How can I gather the rewards of American life while retaining and giving to my children what is important in my own heritage? The times have changed, and new questions, new definitions, provide new goals and pathways for individuals to follow.

Ben's story illustrates a dilemma no longer pervasive in American life: the importance of living by religious principles in a world defined by secular standards and ambitions. Ben's themes dramatically exemplify the tension between the two modes of thought and being. Other informants were less explicit, but most characterized their lives as guided by a "set of higher truths," "religious teachings," "piety," or "moral imperatives," however diffuse. The tension between religious and secular lifestyles and the need to live by "religious truths" are no longer compelling facts of American life, and they have lost their meaning as vital pathways.

The pioneer is, perhaps, the quintessential and original American identity. Stella embodies its characteristics—the independent freethinking person, secure and adventurous enough to go to the limits of her world and make something of herself along the way. As expressed by my informants, assimilation and behavior grounded in religious morality are no longer widespread American goals. More important, they are no longer indispensable to being American. The idea of the pioneer remains, I believe, and is as salient as ever to identity formulation, though the frontiers have changed drastically since the youth of my informants.

My aim has been to broaden and deepen our knowledge of the aging process through the vocabulary of personal reflection and hindsight in the form of the life story. By presenting the voices of individuals, describing themes as the building blocks of identity, and explicating the sources from which themes emerge, I have tried to show the wealth of resources individuals employ to construct a coherent picture of who they are and how their lives have been. These cases illustrate that an individual does not comprehend his or her self as a linear sequence—a succession of roles or a trajectory of gains and losses. Nor do people think of themselves as purely "socialized" beings, learning and then acting out (or deviating from) a set of socially appropriate rules of behavior. Moreover, identity in old age is not merely the sum of the parts, whether roles, achievements, losses, or social norms. Instead, people dynamically integrate a wide range of experience—unique situations, structural forces, values, cultural pathways, knowledge of an entire life span—to construct a current and viable identity.

The key here is integration; this is the heart of the creative, symbolic process of self-formulation in late life. If we can find the sources of meaning held by the elderly and see how individuals put it all together, we will go a long way toward appreciating the complexity of human aging and the ultimate reality of coming to terms with one's whole life.

Appendix

Notes

Bibliography

Index

Appendix

Interview Guide

I have divided the questions into topical areas for presentation here. I asked each of the 15 informants most of these questions. But I did not ask questions in any particular sequence.

LIFE EVENTS

1. When and where were you born?
2. What are your earliest memories? Probes.
3. Did you have any brothers or sisters? Tell me about them.
4. What were your parents doing then?
5. Tell me something else about your childhood. Probes.
6. How would you describe yourself during those years? How would others have described you?
7. Tell me about your adolescence/young adulthood.
8. What were you doing then? What were your concerns? What was that like for you?
9. What happened next?
10. When you think of that time, what stands out in your mind now?
11. How would you describe yourself then? How would others have described you?
12. Tell me about your religious background/training.
13. Tell me about your marriage; first job; leaving home. What were your concerns then? What was that like for you? Probes.
14. Tell me about raising your children.
15. Tell me about your career, occupation. What were you doing in

your 30s, 40s, 50s? How would you describe yourself then? How would others have described you?

16. Who have been the most influential people at various stages in your life? Why? When? What were you doing at that time?
17. How do/did you feel about retirement?

THE PRESENT

1. Could you describe to me a typical day?
2. Who are the people you are closest to now? How often do you see them? How many friends would you say you have now?
3. Mutual aid/reciprocity: To whom would you go for help with: financial aid, housekeeping, transportation, emotional support?

LIFE REVIEW

1. What do you feel have been the important successes in your life? The frustrations?
2. I'm interested in what people see as important turning points in their lives. Could you describe any? What were you doing then? What were you like then?
3. What have been the most influential experiences in your life?
4. Are there periods of your life that you remember more vividly than others? Which ones? Why? What were your concerns at that time?
5. Have there been times in your life when you threw out a lot of stuff? What times? What stuff? Probes.
6. If you were writing the story of your life, how would you divide it into chapters?
7. What sorts of things frighten you now? When you were in your 60s? 50s? 40s? 30s? 20s? A child? Probes.
8. What kinds of things give you the most pleasure now? When you were in your 60s? 50s? 40s? 30s? 20s? A child? Probes.
9. If you could live your whole life over, what would you do differently?

IDENTITY

1. How are you like your mother? Unlike her? How are you like your father? Unlike him?
2. Do you feel differently about yourself now from how you felt when you were younger? How?
3. What is your best quality? Your worst quality?
4. Do you have a philosophy of life? If a young person came to you

asking you what's the most important thing in living a good life, what would you say?

5. What do you think has stayed the same about you throughout life? What do you think has changed?

6. I held a hand mirror up to informants' faces and asked, "What do you see?"

AGING

1. How can one prepare for old age?

2. Did you have any expectations at various points in your life about what growing older would be like for you? What about when your parents grew older?

3. How do you feel about growing old now?

4. If you were going to live 20 more years, what would you do? How would you like that? What plans would you make?

5. What is the hardest thing about growing older? The best thing?

6. Do you think about the future? Make plans? What are your concerns for the future?

7. What do you look forward to now?

8. Do you think about death?

Notes

One: Agelessness, Identity, and Themes

1 For examples, see Cohler 1982; Erikson 1959, 1968; Mortimer et al. 1982; Pearlin 1980.

2 Lutsky (1980) also found that the aged tend to view themselves as younger than their chronological age, unless they are in poor health.

3 See Kroeber and Kluckhohn 1963 for a review of definitions of the term culture. See Geertz 1973 for a more recent definition.

4 See Hazan 1980 and 1984 for both ethnographic and theoretical investigations of the experience of time among the elderly.

5 For example, see Baltes and Willis 1977:142; Elder 1981; Foner 1984.

6 Crapanzano (1984:954) notes that life histories in anthropology are generally seen as "portraying" or "illustrating" some aspect of culture.

7 The concept of "accountable" is taken from Harold Garfinkle, *Studies in Ethnomethodology* (1967). He uses the term to mean that people are "accountable" all the time, in the process of everyday living. ". . . Accounts of everyday activities are used as prescriptions with which to locate, to identify, to analyze, to classify, to make recognizable, or to find one's way around in comparable occasions . . ." (p. 2). I use the term in a more restricted sense; people looking back on their lives are also making sense out of them.

8 See especially Langness and Frank 1981 and Crapanzano 1984 for a discussion of the anthropological literature on this issue. See Lieberman and Tobin 1983 and Nydegger 1980 for a review of related problems from a gerontological perspective.

9 Myerhoff's work (especially 1979 and 1984) employs *ritual*,

story-telling, and *reminiscence* as process variables to portray individual lives and develop gerontological theory. Neugarten (1985) cites the importance of the *autobiographical account* as a variable in understanding life transitions in old age. Brim and Ryff (1980) and others view the *life-event* as the essential variable in human development research.

Two: Themes in the Life Story

1 This approach is taken from Clifford Geertz, *The Interpretation of Cultures* (1973), especially pp. 448–449.
2 I gathered the life stories by bits and pieces, in the context of conversations that covered many topics. Because I did not elicit or collect cohesive texts, and because I was not looking for the meaning of the texts in conjunction with their structure, my analysis is not informed by rules or properties of narrative. A narrative is a style of writing or speaking that contains numerous structural aspects including the following: a preface or introduction, a sequence of events, a cast of characters, a plot, a point and a resolution. A definition of narrative and a detailed example of narrative analysis of an interview appears in Paget 1982. The stories I collected do not contain all these elements, nor were they intended to do so. I did not seek out structural features when analyzing interview materials; neither did I attempt to analyze the development of a concise storyline.
3 I discerned themes from the texts by these methods. Other analysts might discover different themes, or additional ones.
4 I am indebted to David Plath for clarifying these dimensions.
5 Pseudonyms are used throughout this book to preserve anonymity. I have also altered identifying biographical information that does not pertain to themes.
6 See Caudill 1958; Henry 1963; Taylor 1970.
7 David Mandelbaum in "The Study of Life History: Gandhi" (1973:181) discusses "turnings" as the acquisition of new roles and relationships.
8 Eric Pfeiffer, "A Short Portable Mental Status Questionnaire for the Assessment of Organic Brain Deficit in Elderly Patients" (1975). This mental status questionnaire is a standard for assessing cognitive deficits in the elderly. It contains the questions: What is the date today? and What day is it?

Three: Structural Sources of Meaning

1 In *Children of the Great Depression* (1974: 3), Glen H. Elder notes that the period from 1929 to 1933 was not one of great deprivation for at least half the U.S. population.

2 Christie Kiefer discusses the individual's perceived relationship to history and historical processes in *Changing Cultures: Changing Lives* (1974), especially pp. 49–81.

3 A number of longitudinal studies analyze the role played in later life by ego strength acquired much earlier in the life span. See also: Block 1971; Haan and Day 1974; Lowenthal et al. 1975; Maas and Kuypers 1975; Peskin 1972.

4 Twelve informants resided in long-term care facilities during the study period. All others owned and lived in their own homes.

Four: Values as Sources of Meaning

1 I am grateful to Christie Kiefer for his help in clarifying the distinction between "themes" and "values" set forth here. He offered many suggestions which I have incorporated into this chapter.

2 Such as: Arensberg and Niehoff (1975); Epstein (1980); Gorer (1948); Kluckhohn and Kluckhohn (1947); Kluckhohn and Strodtbeck (1961); Lasch (1979); Mead (1943); Williams (1970).

Five: The Ageless Self

1 Psychoanalytic technique does aim to separate the meaning of the past from that of the present. However, free association, rather than the oral life story, is the vehicle used to accomplish that goal.

2 See Mandelbaum (1973) for a discussion and review of this concept.

3 Continuity is discussed at great length in Myerhoff, *Number Our Days* (1979), especially pp. 108–109; 221–222.

4 The active search for continuity may be described as an important adaptive mechanism for the study participants.

5 The idea of maintaining a self-image in which moral worth and social status are achieved is fully elaborated by Niels Braroe in *Indian and White* (1975).

6 Barbara Myerhoff (1979:195–231) describes a similar situation in the case of Jacob Koved.

7 See especially G. Becker 1980; Clark and Anderson 1967; Hochschild 1973; Keith Ross 1977; Myerhoff 1979, 1984; Myerhoff and Simić 1978, and Plath 1980.

Six: Coming to Terms

1 Irving Rosow considers this phenomenon at length in *Socialization to Old Age* (1974).

2 The term "pathways" is taken from David Plath, *Long Engagements* (1980). He refers to pathways as "lifecourse directives for one's self-realization" of cultural values (p. 14). "By midlife we come to a new awareness of time as it flows through *our* life as well as the lives of people in general. We notice a dislocation between our culture's ideal pathways of life and the actual paths we are traveling" (p. 13).

3 "Life plan" is from Robert A. LeVine, "Adulthood among the Gusii of Kenya," in *Themes of Work and Love in Adulthood*, N. J. Smelser and E. H. Erikson, Eds. (1980). "By 'life plan,' I mean a people's collective representation of the life-course viewed as an organized system of shared ideals about how life should be lived and shared expectancies about how lives are lived. My assumption is that every people has a life plan in this sense—it is the normative aspect of their culture viewed from the perspective of the individual—though it is elaborated as explicit ideology in some cultures and not in others" (p. 82).

4 See Zborowski and Herzog's *Life Is with People* (1952), and Barbara Myerhoff's *Number Our Days* (1979) for detailed descriptions of shtetl culture.

Bibliography

Arensberg, Conrad M., and Arthur N. Niehoff. 1975. American Cultural Values. In The Nacirema, J. Spradley and M. A. Rynkiewich, Eds. Boston: Little Brown, pp. 363–378.

Baltes, Paul B., and Sherry L. Willis. 1977. Toward Psychological Theories of Aging and Development. In Handbook of the Psychology of Aging, J. E. Birren and K. W. Schaie, Eds. New York: Van Nostrand Reinhold, pp. 128–154.

Becker, Gaylene. 1980. Growing Old in Silence. Berkeley: University of California Press.

Becker, Howard. 1968a. The Self and Adult Socialization. In The Study of Personality: An Interdisciplinary Appraisal, E. Norbeck, D. Price-Williams, and W. M. McCord, Eds. New York: Holt, Rinehart and Winston, pp. 194–208.

Becker, Howard. 1968b. Personal Change in Adult Life. In Middle Age and Aging, B. Neugarten, Ed. Chicago: University of Chicago Press, pp. 148–158.

Bertaux, Daniel. 1981. Introduction. In Biography and Society, D. Bertaux, Ed. Beverly Hills: Sage, pp. 5–15.

Block, Jack. 1971. Lives through Time. Berkeley: Bancroft Books.

Braroe, Niels Winther. 1975. Indian and White. Stanford: Stanford University Press.

Brim, Orville G., and J. Kagan, Eds. 1980. Constancy and Change in Human Development. Cambridge: Harvard University Press.

Brim, Orville G., Jr., and Carol D. Ryff. 1980. On the Properties of Life Events. In Life-Span Development and Human Behavior, Vol. 2, P. Baltes and O. Brim, Eds. New York: Academic Press, pp. 367–388.

Buhler, Charlotte. 1935. The Curve of Life as Studied in Biographies. Journal of Applied Psychology 19:405–409.

Buhler, Charlotte, and Fred Massarik, Eds. 1968. The Course of Human Life. New York: Springer.

Burke, Kenneth. 1950. A Rhetoric of Motives. Berkeley: University of California Press.

Caudill, William. 1958. The Psychiatric Hospital as a Small Society. Cambridge: Harvard University Press.

Clark, Margaret. 1967. The Anthropology of Aging. A New Area for Studies of Culture and Personality. Gerontologist 7 : 55–64.

Clark, Margaret. 1972. Cultural Values and Dependency in Later Life. In Aging and Modernization, D. O. Cowgill and L. D. Holmes, Eds. New York: Appleton Century Crofts, pp. 263–274.

Clark, Margaret, and Barbara Anderson. 1967. Culture and Aging. Springfield: Charles Thomas.

Cohler, Bertram J. 1982. Personal Narrative and Life Course. In Life-Span Development and Behavior, Vol. 4, P. Baltes and O. Brim, Eds. New York: Academic Press, pp. 205–241.

Crapanzano, Vincent. 1984. Life-Histories. American Anthropologist 86 : 953 960.

Elder, Glen H. 1974. Children of the Great Depression. Chicago: University of Chicago Press.

Elder, Glen H. 1981. History and the Life Course. In Biography and Society, D. Bertaux, Ed. Beverly Hills: Sage, pp. 77–115.

Epstein, Joseph. 1980. Ambition. New York: Dutton.

Erikson, Erik H. 1959. Identity and the Life Cycle. Psychological Issues, Vol. 1, New York: International Universities Press.

Erikson, Erik H. 1963. Childhood and Society. New York: Norton.

Erikson, Erik H. 1968. Identity: Youth and Crisis. New York: Norton.

Erikson, Erik H. 1969. Gandhi's Truth. New York: Norton.

Erikson, Erik H. 1975. On the Nature of "Psycho-Historical" Evidence. In Life History and the Historical Moment. New York: Norton, pp. 113–168.

Erikson, Erik H. 1976. Reflections on Dr. Borg's Life Cycle. Daedalus, Spring: 1–28.

Featherman, David L. 1983. Life-Span Perspectives in Social Science Research. In Life-Span Development and Behavior, Vol. 5, P. Baltes and O. Brim, Eds. New York: Academic Press, pp. 1–57.

Foner, Nancy. 1984. Age and Social Change. In Age and Anthropological Theory, D. Kertzer and J. Keith, Eds. Ithaca: Cornell University Press, pp. 195–216.

Garfinkel, Harold. 1967. Studies in Ethnomethodology. Englewood Cliffs: Prentice-Hall.

Geertz, Clifford. 1973. The Interpretation of Cultures. New York: Basic Books.

Glaser, Barney. 1978. Theoretical Sensitivity. Mill Valley: Sociology Press.

Glaser, Barney, and Anselm Strauss. 1967. The Discovery of Grounded Theory. Chicago: Aldine.

Goffman, Erving. 1959. The Presentation of Self in Everyday Life. New York: Anchor Books.

Goffman, Erving. 1974. Frame Analysis. New York: Harper and Row.

Gorer, Geoffrey. 1948. The American People: A Study in National Character. New York: Norton.

Haan, Norma, and David Day. 1974. A Longitudinal Study of Change and Sameness in Personality Development. Aging and Human Development 5 : 11 – 39.

Hallowell, A. Irving. 1955. Culture and Experience. Philadelphia: University of Pennsylvania Press.

Hareven, Tamara, Ed. 1978a. Themes in the History of the Family. Charlottesville: University Press of Virginia.

Hareven, Tamara, Ed. 1978b. Transition: The Family and the Life Course in Historical Perspectives. New York: Academic Press.

Hazan, Haim. 1980. The Limbo People: A Study of the Constitution of the Time Universe among the Aged. London: Routledge and Kegan Paul.

Hazan, Haim. 1984. Continuity and Transformation among the Aged: A Study in the Anthropology of Time. Current Anthropology 25 : 567 – 578.

Hellman, Lillian. 1974. Pentimento. New York: Signet.

Henry, Jules. 1963. Culture against Man. New York: Random House.

Hochschild, Arlie. 1973. The Unexpected Community. Berkeley: University of California Press.

Hsu, Francis L. K. 1972. American Core Value and National Character. In Psychological Anthropology, F. L. K. Hsu, Ed. Cambridge: Schenkman, New edition, pp. 241 – 262.

Hutchins, Robert Maynard, Ed. in Chief. 1952. Great Books of the Western World. Chicago: Encyclopedia Britannica, 54 volumes.

Jung, Carl G. 1963. Modern Man in Search of a Soul. New York: Harcourt Brace and World.

Keith Ross, Jennie. 1977. Old People, New Lives. Chicago: University of Chicago Press.

Kiefer, Christie W. 1974. Changing Cultures, Changing Lives. San Francisco: Jossey-Bass.

Kluckhohn, Clyde. 1951. Values and Value-Orientations in the Theory of Action. In Toward a General Theory of Action, T. Parsons and E. A. Shils, Eds. Cambridge: Harvard University Press, pp. 388–433.

Kluckhohn, Clyde, and Florence Kluckhohn. 1947. American Culture: Generalized Orientations and Class Patterns. In Conflicts of Power in Modern Culture. Symposium of Conference in Science, Philosophy, and Religion. New York.

Kluckhohn, Florence. 1953. Dominant and Variant Value Orientations. In Personality in Nature, Society, and Culture, C. Kluckhohn and H. A. Murray, Eds. New York: Alfred A. Knopf. Second edition, revised and enlarged, pp. 342–357.

Kluckhohn, Florence, and Fred L. Strodtbeck. 1961. Variations in Value Orientations. Evanston: Row, Peterson.

Kohlberg, Lawrence. 1964. Development of Moral Character and Moral Ideology. In Review of Child Development Research, M. L. Hoffman and L. W. Hoffman, Eds. New York: Russell Sage Foundation, pp. 383–432.

Kotre, John N. 1984. Outliving the Self: Generativity and the Interpretation of Lives. Baltimore: Johns Hopkins University Press.

Kroeber, A. L., and Clyde Kluckhohn. 1963. Culture: A Critical Review of Concepts and Definitions. New York: Vintage Books.

Langness, L. L., and Gelya Frank. 1981. Lives: An Anthropological Approach to Biography. Novato: Chandler and Sharp.

Lasch, Christopher. 1979. The Culture of Narcissism. New York: Warner Books.

LeVine, Robert A. 1980. Adulthood among the Gusii of Kenya. In Themes of Work and Love in Adulthood, N. Smelser and E. Erikson, Eds. Cambridge: Harvard University Press.

Lieberman, Morton, and Sheldon Tobin. 1983. The Experience of Old Age. New York: Basic Books.

Loevinger, Jane. 1966. The Meaning and Measurement of Ego Development. American Psychologist 21: 195–206.

Lowenthal, Marjorie Fiske, Majda Thurnher, and David Chiriboga. 1975. Four Stages of Life. San Francisco: Jossey-Bass.

Lutsky, Neil S. 1980. Attitudes toward Old Age and Elderly Persons. In Annual Review of Gerontology and Geriatrics, Vol. 1, C. Eisdorfer, Ed. New York: Springer.

Maas, Henry S., and Joseph A. Kuypers. 1975. From Thirty to Seventy. San Francisco: Jossey-Bass.

Maddox, George. 1968. Persistence of Life Style among the Elderly: A Longitudinal Study of Patterns of Social Activity in Relation to Life Satisfaction. In Middle Age and Aging, B. Neugarten, Ed. Chicago: University of Chicago Press, pp. 181–184.

Maddox, George, and James Wiley. 1976. Scope, Concepts and Methods in the Study of Aging. In Handbook of Aging and the Social Sciences, R. H. Binstock and E. Shanas, Eds. New York: Van Nostrand Reinhold, pp. 3–34.

Mandelbaum, David G. 1973. The Study of Life History: Gandhi. Current Anthropology 14 : 177–196.

Mead, George Herbert. 1934. Mind, Self and Society. Chicago: University of Chicago Press.

Mead, Margaret. 1943. And Keep Your Powder Dry: An Anthropologist Looks at America. New York: Morrow.

Mortimer, Jeylan T., Michael D. Finch, and Donald Kumka. 1982. Persistence and Change in Development: The Multidimensional Self-Concept. In Life-Span Development and Behavior, Vol. 4, P. Baltes and O. Brim, Eds. New York: Academic Press, pp. 263–313.

Myerhoff, Barbara. 1979. Number Our Days. New York: E. P. Dutton.

Myerhoff, Barbara. 1984. Rites and Signs of Ripening: The Intertwining of Ritual, Time, and Growing Older. In Age and Anthropological Theory, D. Kertzer and J. Keith, Eds. Ithaca: Cornell University Press, pp. 305–330.

Myerhoff, Barbara, and Andrei Simić, Eds. 1978. Life's Career—Aging. Beverly Hills: Sage.

Neugarten, Bernice L., Ed. 1968. Middle Age and Aging. Chicago: University of Chicago Press.

Neugarten, Bernice L. 1977. Personality and Aging. In Handbook of the Psychology of Aging, J. E. Birren and K. W. Schaie, Eds. New York: Van Nostrand Reinhold, pp. 626–649.

Neugarten, Bernice L. 1985. Interpretive Social Science and Research on Aging. In Gender and the Life Course, A. S. Rossi, Ed. American Sociological Association Presidential Volume, New York: Aldine, pp. 291–300.

Nydegger, Corinne. 1980. Role and Age Transitions: A Potpourri of Issues. In New Methods for Old Age Research, C. Frye and J. Keith, Eds. Chicago: Loyola University Press.

Opler, Morris. 1945. Themes and Dynamic Forces in Culture. American Journal of Sociology 51 : 198–205.

Paget, Marianne A. 1982. Your Son Is Cured Now; You May Take Him Home. Culture Medicine and Psychiatry 6 : 237–259.

Pearlin, Leonard. 1980. Life Strains and Psychological Distress among Adults. In Themes of Work and Love in Adulthood, N. Smelser and E. Erikson, Eds. Cambridge: Harvard University Press, pp. 174–192.

Peskin, H. 1972. Multiple Prediction of Adult Psychological Health and Preadolescent and Adolescent Behavior. Journal of Consulting and Clinical Psychology 38:155–160.

Pfeiffer, Eric. 1975. A Short Portable Mental Status Questionnaire for the Assessment of Organic Brain Deficit in Elderly Patients. Journal of American Geriatrics Society 23:433–441.

Plath, David. 1980. Long Engagements. Stanford: Stanford University Press.

Rosow, Irving. 1974. Socialization to Old Age. Berkeley: University of California Press.

Ryff, Carol D. 1984. Personality Development from the Inside: The Subjective Experience of Change in Adulthood and Aging. In Life-Span Development and Behavior, Vol. 6, P. Baltes and O. Brim, Eds. New York: Academic Press, pp. 243–279.

Scott-Maxwell, Florida. 1978. The Measure of My Days. New York: Alfred A. Knopf.

Simić, Andrei. 1978. Introduction: Aging and the Aged in Cultural Perspective. In Life's Career—Aging, B. Myerhoff and A. Simić, Eds. Beverly Hills: Sage, pp. 9–22.

Taylor, Carol. 1970. In Horizontal Orbit: Hospitals and the Cult of Efficiency. New York: Holt, Rinehart and Winston.

Watson, Lawrence C. 1976. Understanding a Life History as a Subjective Document. Ethos 4:95–131.

Williams, Robin M., Jr. 1970. American Society: A Sociological Interpretation. New York: Alfred A. Knopf. Third edition, revised.

Zborowski, Mark, and Elizabeth Herzog. 1952. Life Is with People. New York: International Universities Press.

Index